RAY HAMILTON

summersdale

THE JOY OF GOLF

Summersdale Publishers Ltd
46 West Street
Chichester
West Sussex
PO19 1RP
UK

www.summersdale.com

Printed and bound in the Czech Republic

ISBN: 978-1-84953-598-4

Substantial discounts on bulk quantities of Summersdale books are available to corporations, professional associations and other organisations. For details contact Nicky Douglas by telephone: +44 (0) 1243 756902, fax: +44 (0) 1243 786300 or email: nicky@summersdale.com.

Acknowledgements

My thanks once more to all at Summersdale Publishers (IPG Trade Publisher of the Year 2014!) for the opportunity and support to write this book on a subject dear to my heart, and in particular to Chris Turton for yet more excellent editing ideas and to Claire Cock-Starkey for her careful and patient copy-editing.

To everyone who has ever had the misfortune to watch me play golf, thank you for your patience. It all started with my father many moons ago and it continues to this day with friends, family and the itinerant Mayfield Golfing Society. I dedicate this book to you all.

CONTENTS

INTRODUCTION

*Golf is so popular simply because it is the best
game in the world at which to be bad.*

A. A. MILNE, ENGLISH AUTHOR AND 18-HANDICAP GOLFER

Golf is one of the world's greatest sports, and one of the most popular, which is perhaps surprising when you consider how difficult it is to play. It involves accurately hitting a relatively small ball as few times as possible around a long-distance, open-air obstacle course, with the aim of sinking that small ball down 18 different small holes; it involves postures and movements that do not sit naturally with the basic design of the human body (you need only think of the way you grip a golf club to realise this); and it involves a superhuman strength of mind over matter as soon as you are playing for anything other than fun (just think of the difference between any putt on the practice green and the need to hole out from ten feet to win a competition).

So what makes it so popular in the face of these physical and mental challenges? Is it simply because we relish an opportunity to overcome life's obstacles? Is it because, in common with our ancestors, we feel the need to walk the earth and breathe the air before retreating to our shelters for the night? Is it that golf has always enjoyed a certain prestige, a level of composed dignity that other sports do not display? Could it be that we simply yearn for the euphoria that is experienced from the transient success of the well-flighted ball or the perfectly judged putt, that one shot that looks as if it could just as easily have been played by Rory McIlroy at Augusta National? Or does golf primarily serve as a means to enjoy the camaraderie that comes with a social gathering of like-minded people? It is popular, of course, for all of those reasons.

Golf as we know it today had humble Scottish beginnings around 600 years ago, but it has long since gone global, becoming a multi-billion pound industry as more and more people took up the game after seeing their heroes win major tournaments on TV, or because they were drawn into the sport by already-addicted friends or family members.

I personally had no choice but to be interested in golf. For one thing, I was born in Scotland. For another thing, my father was a member of Elderslie Golf Club in Renfrewshire, where he enlisted me as a junior member at a very early age. Apparently, I showed promise, which I have yet to realise some decades later. Such was my father's passion for the game that he ultimately bought a house overlooking Elderslie's fourth green and fifth tee, and it was not unknown for us to sneak onto the fifth tee before the sun was up over the horizon, still somewhat wobbly from the session that had taken place in the clubhouse 200 yards along the path only hours before.

I have played golf for so many years that I have probably experienced first hand most of what the game has to offer: joy, pain, disbelief, ecstasy, humiliation, camaraderie, that winning feeling, that losing feeling, confidence, a lack of confidence, fresh air, very fresh air, rain, sunshine, even snow and ice.

I have been lucky enough to play (badly) some of the great courses (St Andrews, Wentworth, the Belfry, Gleneagles, to name but four), and to have played in many different countries across the continents of the world, but most of my fun has been had playing at a more relaxed level with family and friends and fellow members of the Mayfield Golfing Society.

I have also played golf long enough to understand a thing or two about temperament. As a young man, I would bludgeon my own head with a 5-iron for failing to hit the green on a hole that I had made par on the week before, simply because I knew I had the skill to do it again. As a less young man, my temperament has improved to the extent that I can appreciate the good shots for what they are (mostly luck) and be philosophical about the increasing number of 'unlucky' ones. But I still have a lot of fun trying to hit a ball with a stick into a hole.

If you too enjoy hitting balls with sticks, or even if you just enjoy watching the pros do it properly on the telly, this book should grip you from the start, keep you hooked to the end, and stop your golfing memories from fading. It may even be on a par with your expectations. You have been *fore!* warned.

Note: To the best of my knowledge, the facts and figures in this book are correct as at the end of March 2014.

IN THE BEGINNING THERE WAS *GOWF*

*Columbus went around the world in 1492. That isn't
a lot of strokes when you consider the course.*

Lee Trevino, Mexican-American winner of six majors

Gowf *in the Land of the Heather*

It is widely believed that golf originated in Scotland. Some say that
the word itself derives from the Dutch *colf*, meaning 'stick' or 'club',
and that the Dutch, therefore, must have been the first people to
enjoy hitting something with a stick. Others claim that the ancient
Chinese game of *chuiwan* involved hitting *(chui)* a small ball *(wan)*
'while walking'. Be all that as it may, there seems little doubt that golf
as we know and love it today, played with a set of clubs over 18 holes,
started in the Land of the Heather. The first recorded mention of the
modern game is in a 1471 parliamentary act, in which James II of
Scotland prohibited the playing of golf and football because they
were considered to interfere with his troops' archery practice (and
they probably had a war with England coming up – they usually did
back then).

The oldest still-playing purpose-built golf course in the world is Musselburgh Links near Edinburgh, with documentary evidence that golf was played there in 1672 ('links' courses were so called because it was the Scots word for 'coastal sand dunes'). The 'home of golf', though, is recognised today as the Royal and Ancient Golf Club of St Andrews. Formed in 1754 as The Society of St Andrews Golfers, its status grew with the royal patronage of King William IV in 1834 and the responsibility that came with its codification of the rules of golf in 1897.

Fore!

For the chop

In a very early twist to the countless 'golf widow' jokes that were to follow in the centuries ahead, Mary, Queen of Scots, came under criticism in 1567 for playing golf within a few days of the murder of her husband, Lord Darnley (a murder which she herself is widely believed to have had a hand in). My view is that if she had the tee booked, she had the tee booked. When Mary herself was finally executed in 1587, her last thoughts may well have been along the lines of: This is ironic. I spent all these years trying to have a single stroke cut from my handicap…

Conquering England and beyond

Golf first moved south when King James VI of Scotland also became King James I of England, following the death of Elizabeth I in 1603. The vast Scottish court that travelled south with James was soon playing golf regularly on Blackheath in south-east London. For that reason, although it has only been on its present site in Eltham since 1923, the Royal Blackheath Golf Club is considered to be one of the oldest golf institutions in the world. The oldest golf *course* in England (founded in 1864) is the Royal North Devon at Westward Ho!

It took almost 300 years for golf to really catch on outside of Scotland, but catch on it most certainly did. During the nineteenth century all things Scottish were popularised by the annual visits of Queen Victoria to Balmoral, and golf in particular was brought to the attention of the wider world. By the end of the nineteenth century, clubs were suddenly springing up across England and Ireland (the oldest club in Ireland is the Royal Belfast, founded in 1881). The game had also spread across continental Europe for the benefit of British visitors, and throughout the British Empire for the benefit of British expats. It grew in countries as far-flung as India, Canada, Australia and South Africa. The Royal Calcutta Golf Club had pre-empted the rush in 1829 and is the oldest golf club outside the British Isles, while the Pau Golf Club (1856) in south-west France is the oldest in continental Europe.

Across the pond

Although there is evidence of golf having been played in South Carolina and Georgia in the eighteenth century, the first recognised golf club in the USA is the St Andrew's Golf Club in Yonkers, New York, which kicked off with three holes in 1888. The Chicago Golf Club was the first in the States to achieve an 18-hole course, in 1893. These two clubs, along with Shinnecock Hills on Long Island, Newport Country Club in Rhode Island and The Country Club at Brookline, Massachusetts, were the five founding members of the United States Golf Association in 1894.

With no shortage of real estate to restrict the world's new golfing pioneers, golf clubs popped up like mushrooms across America in the twentieth century, a century in which their professional players would largely dominate the world game. The most famous American club is the Augusta National in Georgia, which opened for business in 1933 and has been home to the US Masters every year since 1934 (except 1943–1945, when World War Two got in the way). The Americans' enthusiasm for the game shows little sign of waning in the twenty-first century and over half the golf courses in the world are now stateside.

Fore!

On the head of population, Jimmy!
The country with the most golf courses per head of population, perhaps appropriately, remains Scotland, followed by New Zealand, Australia, Republic of Ireland and Northern Ireland.

Going Japanese

The Kobe Golf Club is the oldest in Japan, built in 1903 to keep the British expat community amused. Strict rules continue today to maintain its pristine condition, including a limit of eight clubs per player, carried by caddies in canvas bags. The first course opened by the native Japanese, in 1913, was the Tokyo Golf Club at Komazawa, but the playing experience was a bit different to that of the West. Retired Samurai warriors reportedly served as course marshals (slow play was not an issue on that course), giggling geishas served as ball retrievers from the heated water hazards, and Zen monks calmly raked the sand bunkers.

Golf for the masses, however, came late to Japan and the rest of the Far East, not least because of anti-Western sentiment in the first half of the twentieth century, followed by the occupation by Allied forces after World War Two. But recent decades have seen a staggering level of growth, to the extent that there are now probably more courses in Japan than in any other country in the world outside America. And yet, demand continues to outstrip supply, especially for golf-hungry city residents who can't afford to play at the exclusive country clubs, resulting in a proliferation of state-of-the-art multi-tiered driving ranges. For many Japanese golfers, these ranges are the nearest thing to playing golf they will ever experience.

Fore!

To lunch or to lunch, that is the question

The custom of stopping for lunch after nine holes is mandatory at most Japanese golf clubs. When you book, you will be given two tee times – one for the front nine and one for the back nine – with a 45-minute break scheduled in between to enjoy your favourite rice dish washed down with a couple of Asahi beers. (I don't think many golfers would have a problem with that!)

The modern age

Golf in the modern age has brought us new heroes with each generation and has courted worldwide popularity and saturated media coverage. It has provided us with increasingly precise equipment and hi-tech clothing for all seasons, and we are spoilt for choice when it comes to golf courses to play on.

The glory and financial reward that comes with success in increasingly competitive tournaments has bred a new standard of professional golfer, one that seeks to combine athletic prowess with psychological strength. Celebrities with time on their hands have taken to the game like ducks to water, many of them in support of charitable foundations who reap the benefits of the pro-am celebrity circuit.

Golf has been with us long enough now to infiltrate our culture, to appear in our literature and films. The game is awash with tales of sporting triumph and tragedy, with humorous anecdotes, with weird and wonderful episodes. It has evolved its own language of jargon and a comprehensive set of rules and etiquette. The following chapters will canter through all of that and much more besides.

CHAPTER 2

STICKS, BALLS AND OTHER EQUIPMENT

Golf is a game whose aim is to hit a very small ball into a small hole, with weapons singularly ill-designed for the purpose.

WINSTON CHURCHILL, WARTIME LEADER AND AVERAGE GOLFER

It is fair to say that golf equipment in the early days of the game was fairly rudimentary compared to the scientifically tested clubs and balls of today. Next time you find yourself complaining about the lie of your perfectly round ball, or moaning that your customised irons aren't as 'forgiving' as you had been led to believe they would be, try hitting a pebble around a windy sand dune with a stick for a few hours. Here is some history to make you feel grateful for what you've got:

Sticks

1600s: Golf clubs started as all-wooden affairs, with ash or hazel used for the shaft, and beech or fruit woods favoured for the heads. The making of these wooden clubs was to prove a useful sideline for many carpenters and bow makers.

1700s: As golf balls became harder over the years, this meant they could also be thwacked harder. An iron-headed club was introduced, 'rutted' at the bottom to allow playing out of holes and scrapes in the ground, so now blacksmiths got a nice little sideline as well. But clubs remained mostly wooden and master carpenters continued to produce beautifully designed and perfectly balanced examples, many of which can still be admired in museums today (including the British Golf Museum in St Andrews and the USGA [United States Golf Association] Museum in Far Hills, New Jersey).

1800s: This was the century in which wooden clubs were upgraded to hickory shafts and persimmon heads, both woods being imported from America. Most players would have up to nine different types of wooden club in their caddies' hands (golf bags wouldn't be invented until the turn of the twentieth century):

- Two 'play clubs' (long drivers with 45-inch shafts), lest one should be broken during play.
- A 'grass driver' (for use on the fairway).
- Two or three 'spoons' of varying angles for use on or just off the fairway.
- A 'niblick' for use in heavier rough.
- A 'driving putter' for long approach shots into the wind.
- An 'approach putter' with a lofted face for shorter shots to the green.
- A 'green putter' for, well, putting on the green.

These were generally long-nosed clubs with weights set into their heels for balance, but the fairway woods soon started to be replaced with more convex 'bulgers'. Those fitted with brass sole plates to protect them from the hard ground of the links were known as 'brassies'.

As the century wore on, iron clubs, known as 'cleeks', became increasingly popular and it was ultimately possible to play without a single wooden club if you so preferred. The discerning cleek player could select from the following:

- A 'driving iron' (which has made something of a comeback in recent years).
- A 'mid iron' (today's 3-iron).
- Two or three 'mashies' with different lofts (today's 4-, 5- and 6-irons).
- A 'mashie niblick' (for use in bunkers or deep grass).
- A 'rut niblick' (for getting the ball out of scrapes and holes).
- An 'anti-shank iron' (speaks for itself).
- A 'mammoth niblick' (for playing from near impossible rough).

1900s: Durable, rigid steel shafts entered the world of golf in the early twentieth century, being used for 'irons' and for a bewildering array of putters, including 'round', 'square', 'triangular', 'mallet' and 'hammer'. Steel had the huge advantage of being able to be mass produced in factories, and it was responsible therefore for making golf more affordable to the masses.

By the 1970s space-age graphite was found to combine strength with flexibility across the range of 'irons' and rigid steel fell from grace, although lighter-weight steel has returned the alloy to favour in more recent years.

By the 1980s even 'woods' were becoming 'metals', and huge lightweight titanium heads were whipped through the air on the ends of ever-lighter graphite shafts. Titanium also allowed clubfaces to be thinner, increasing the spring-like effect on impact and, theoretically, making the ball fly further (although I can assure you that it is quite possible to make the ball fly not very far at all with the springiest, thinnest metals known to man).

2000s: With all that technology at our disposal, it is not surprising that we entered the twenty-first century with zirconium drivers, with putters made of ceramic or silicon nitride, with a selection of space-age 'hybrid' clubs in our bags.

In their attempts to maintain a relatively level playing field in the face of all this modern technology, the golfing powers-that-be have now restricted club-head size to 'huge' (460 cubic centimetres) and clubface springiness to 'very springy indeed' (if you really want to know, they refer to this as a maximum coefficient of restitution of 0.83).

Those restrictions won't stop golf manufacturers hailing incremental changes as the wonder cure for all your golfing ills – that's why they describe irons as 'forgiving' and extol the virtues of 'rescue' clubs. All you have to do with a hybrid rescue club, apparently, is swing it like a metal wood and stand back and watch it perform like a perfectly struck 1-iron. What could possibly go wrong?

Balls

1400s to 1500s: Once Scots had tired of hitting pebbles with a stick, they tried hitting wooden balls with wooden clubs, but those very expensive clubs and balls soon got damaged and only the very rich could afford to keep replacing them.

1618: Progress came with the introduction of the 'featherie', a thin leather bag stuffed with a top-hat-full of chicken or goose feathers, then painted white. It didn't fly very far, but it flew further than pebbles or solid wood.

1848: In a moment of divine inspiration, the Reverend Robert Adams Paterson came up with the gutta-percha ball. It was made from the milky sap of the Malaysian sapodilla tree and its rubbery consistency would, properly struck, fly over 200 yards.

1898: The Haskell ball (after inventor Coburn Haskell of Cleveland, Ohio) provided the next big breakthrough at the turn of the century. It was an inner rubber core wound with layers of rubber thread and covered in a shell made from the sap of the balata tree native to Central and South America, and it flew further and truer than the gutta-percha.

1905: After players started to notice that their smooth golf balls travelled further once they got a bit old and scarred, they started pitting them from new with whatever tools they had lying around in their sheds. This resulted in ball manufacturers trying a variety of patterns to satisfy the demand for roughed up balls, including the bramble, the mesh and the reverse mesh, until, in 1905, William Taylor designed the dimpled pattern that remains with us today.

1930s: There were many variations in size and weight until standards were introduced in the 1930s, but the standards were different on either side of the Atlantic. Our American cousins hit bigger balls than we did until the world finally standardised on the American regulations for weight (1.62 ounces/45.93 grams), diameter (1.68 inches/42.67 millimetres) and maximum permitted velocity (250 feet/76.2 metres per second, since you ask).

1960s: New synthetic resins and urethane blends were used to improve the durability of golf balls, which continued to be made in layers of different materials until Spalding finally produced the first solid core with a new chemically engineered resin in 1967.

2000s: Continual improvements in the materials used and in the manufacturing process have led us to the happy situation we find ourselves in today, able to choose between 'soft' and 'hard' balls depending on how much we want to 'squeeze' the ball on impact, or 'feel' the shot, or fly the ball further, or land the ball 'softer'.

Fore!

The Dunlop 65

This iconic ball was so called because it commemorated Englishman Henry Cotton's score of 65 in the second round of the Open Championship at Royal St George's in Sandwich, Kent in 1934. He went on to win the first of his three Open titles that year and his 65, a tournament record at the time, was described by the press as 'the perfect round'.

Tees

1400s to 1800s: A pile of sand served perfectly well as a golf tee in the early days of links golf, what with sand being readily available on every single hole.

1889: The first portable golf tee (the 'Bloxsom/Douglas') was constructed. Made of rubber, it had three vertical prongs to hold the ball in place and it sat on, not in, the ground.

1892: Technology went a step further with the 'Perfectum', a rubber tee on a metal spike that was pegged into the ground to hold it steady.

1897: The 'Perfectum' was perfected when the similarly designed 'Victor' tee included a cup-shaped top to cradle the ball as it awaited impact.

1920s: Wooden or plastic tees became the modern choice and started to sell in their gazillions around the world in many shapes, sizes and colours.

2000s: The 'castle' variety is popular because you don't have to remember how far to stick it into the ground, the 'zero-friction' tee will gain you inches on every drive, and cornstarch biodegradable tees served in a reusable mesh bag will leave you feeling really good about yourself.

Gadgets and gizmos

Nowadays, apart from the obvious need for a golf bag in which to carry or transport your sticks, balls and tees, you can also spend huge sums of money on not-quite-so-necessary-but-jolly-useful-nonetheless gadgets and gizmos. Clubs can be transported on remote-controlled battery-operated trolleys, with or without seating. Distance-measuring devices allow you to dispense with mind-eye coordination – human eyesight is becoming so last century. In the USA, you can spend $60,000 on a 'golf cart hovercraft', which completely does away with the need to travel round bunkers, ponds, lakes and even other golfers. Although you won't be able to use them in competitions, you could treat yourself to golf balls that transmit radio signals and/or flash until you find them. Extendable ball retrievers mean you will never again have to swim in freezing cold ponds in the middle of winter to save the cost of a new ball, and golf ball picker-ups attached to the top of your putter mean you will never again have to bend down to pick your ball out of the hole (just don't ever lend the picker-up to my mate Tim Gorringe – you'll never see it again).

RULES, ETIQUETTE AND JARGON

If you think it's hard to meet new people,
try picking up the wrong golf ball.

JACK LEMMON, AMERICAN ACTOR

It's complicated!

A game as complicated as golf requires a complicated set of rules, and that is exactly what it has been given. But golf is also a social game, which means that good form with your fellow players is equally important – as such, golf has also been given a complicated etiquette. But complicated rules and etiquette cannot be properly applied without the jargon required to express serious things in a straightforward and, preferably, humorous way, so golf has also developed a colourful vocabulary. This jargon has the added benefit of not allowing non-golfers to know what golfers are talking about, but has the unfortunate side effect of not allowing golfers to know what other golfers are talking about.

Them's the rules (olden days)

The oldest surviving rules of golf were written in 1744 for the Company of Gentlemen Golfers, who played at Leith Links near Edinburgh. They included the following:

If a Ball be stopp'd by any person, Horse, Dog, or any thing else, The Ball so stopp'd must be play'd, where it lyes. You are not to remove Stones, Bones or any Break Club, for the sake of playing your Ball, Except upon the fair Green & that only within a Club's length of your Ball.

If your Ball comes among Watter or any wattery filth, you are at liberty to take out your Ball & bringing it behind the hazard and Teeing it you may play it with any Club and allow your Adversary a Stroke for so getting out your Ball.

If you draw your Club in order to Strike & proceed so far in the Stroke as to be bringing down your Club; If then, your Club shall break in any way, it is to be Accounted a Stroke.

I imagine that golfing tales of woe back then might have gone something like: 'I would have won that match if yon horse hadn't picked up my ball and set it down in the wattery filth.' Or perhaps: 'And then I went and broke my niblick on that dead man's bones. Should old Angus not have been buried by now anyway?'

Them's the rules (nowadays)

Today's rules are jointly approved by the R & A (the name being derived from the Royal and Ancient Golf Club) and the USGA. The R & A operates on behalf of the golfing world but the USGA has the final say in the USA and Mexico so that they can have rules there relating to sand traps instead of bunkers and talk about the need to practice, not practise, their shots.

The rules tell players what they are and are not allowed to do, e.g. what they should do in the face of movable obstructions, immovable obstructions and loose impediments; what to do if a ball in motion gets deflected or stopped by a player or by golf equipment; how balls should be replaced or substituted in different circumstances; how many clubs they are allowed to have in their bag (14).

Fore!

Rule 19-2

Many of the rules of golf exist to tell players what to do in unusual situations. Let's say you hit your ball into a nearby tree and it rebounds on to your head at great speed. A quick glance at Rule 19-2 will tell you that you should rub salt into your bulging head wound by penalising yourself one stroke for having stopped a ball in motion with your body. You must then play your next shot as it lies, unless maybe it deflected off your head and into another player's trouser pocket. Again, reference to Rule 19-2 makes it clear that you are allowed to remove the ball from a player's clothing before next thrashing into it with an iron. This is an important rule to know.

Etiquette

This is about showing respect for the course you are playing and the other golfers on it. It is also about keeping golf safe and enjoyable. Some of the rules of etiquette are really rather obvious (replace your divots, repair your pitch marks, rake bunkers after playing out of them, don't make a noise or move about when somebody else is playing a shot, keep up with the group ahead, don't walk on the line of another player's putt, etc, etc, etc) but it is surprising how many 'offences' are committed every single day on golf courses around the world. Perhaps we should be increasingly philosophical about those offences as golf becomes increasingly popular, but I have written to my MP anyway to test the waters on whether hanging might be brought back for inconsiderate golfers.

Etiquette is, by its very nature, a thing of tradition, but sometimes even traditions have to be brought up to date to fit with the modern world we live in. Here are my top etiquette tips for the twenty-first century:

- Don't make phone calls except in an emergency, e.g. if a player in the group ahead has been attacked by a pack of wild dogs and you need a ruling on whether you should ring for an ambulance or play through as if nothing had happened.

- Don't tweet your way round the course. Most of your Twitter followers will think you're a halfwit if you post an account of each and every golf shot you play.

- Don't waste time taking selfies to prove on Facebook that you're playing a nice golf course. Most people don't care, not even your Facebook 'close friends'.

- Don't even think that you can multitask to the extent of composing a text message while you walk between shots. Predictive text thrives on phrases like 'loose chip shot'.

- Don't use your GPS distance finder standing next to a 150-yard marker. Just ask your playing partners if any of them know how far it is from the 150-yard marker to the middle of the green – they will be more than pleased to help you out with that.

It is good sportsmanship not to pick up lost balls while they are still rolling.

MARK TWAIN, AMERICAN AUTHOR

Jargon

Most golfers have become so accustomed to the jargon of the game that they no longer recognise it as jargon. Professional, amateur and club golfers alike will discuss how they 'made double bogey' or 'narrowly missed for eagle', and will feel no need to explain that a 'birdie' is one under the regulation par for the hole, or that being 'dormie two' means that they are two holes ahead of their match-play opponent with two holes to play and cannot therefore lose the match they are playing. It is a very specific language which adds colour, and very often humour, to an otherwise serious game.

But imagine for a moment that you don't know the first thing about golf and you've just wandered into a clubhouse while the following conversation is going on:

'After being five over at the turn, I nearly eagled the dogleg tenth after I drew a punched 2-iron on the Tiger line right over the fairway bunker. The little beauty just missed the rough on the left, bounced once on the apron and rolled nicely on to the dance floor, finishing up pin-high, thank you very much. I thought the putt was going to drop in the back door after running round the cup, but I was happy with the gimme for a birdie anyway.'

As confusing as that may sound to a non-golfer, there is absolutely nothing unusual about that conversation if you play the game and, just to show that you can jargon with the best of them, you might reply along the following lines:

'Nice one, Pedro, but you always were a jammy dodger. I wouldn't be surprised if you'd stuck your approach straight in for an albatross in the first place.'

Even to the seasoned 'jargonist', however, there are some terms that remain quite rare in the world of golf-speak, or which may have fallen from favour with the passage of time. Here are some examples:

Condor: What you get if you score a triple eagle, i.e. a hole-in-one on a par five or a two on a par six. Only four have ever been recorded.

 Cuban: A ball that stops just short of the hole, i.e. because it needed just one more revolution.

 Dog licence: A match-play defeat by the margin of 7 & 6 (because the cost of a dog licence pre-decimalisation was seven shillings and sixpence).

 Golden ferret: When you hole out from a bunker.

 James Joyce: A putt that's difficult to read.

 Ostrich: A score of five under par on a single hole, i.e. a hole-in-one on a par six. This has never been achieved and never will be.

 Snowman: To score eight (i.e. the shape of a snowman) on a single hole (this is much more common than an ostrich).

 Turkey: Three consecutive birdies in the same round, i.e. three birdies 'on the trot'.

 Vaulting dormie: Occurs in match play when a player wins without passing through 'dormie' (which is a guaranteed tie at the end of play). For example, going from 'one up' with two to play to 'two up' with one to play.

CHAPTER 4

LOOKING
THE PART

Although golf was originally restricted to wealthy Protestants,
today it's open to anybody who owns hideous clothing.

DAVE BARRY, AMERICAN HUMOURIST

A matter of taste

Golf is largely an individual game, which allows for a degree of individual style, but that is not to say that certain trends have not prevailed down the centuries. From Harris tweed to Gore-Tex, from heavy wool to breathable membrane, let us admire the golfing fashions of the ages, with the odd nod to those who would set the trends and those who would seem determined to buck them.

Down the ages

Olden times

Notwithstanding any misconceptions that early red-bearded Scots golfers might have played in kilts and recently slaughtered animal skins, golf clothing was in fact pretty functional from the start, with players sporting heavy Harris tweed jackets and caps, tartan 'troosers', sturdy brogues and some thick socks from the woollen mill up the road. Basically, anything heavy enough to keep out the winds that blasted off the sea onto the links courses.

Not-quite-so-olden times

As the game slowly moved south to the refined English, the emphasis became more on looking smart and functionality be damned, Sir! This was, after all, a game played by royalty and by gentlemen. Tailcoats with knee-length breeches, also known as knickerbockers, were the order of the day. The Scots could do nothing but stand back and admire their more fashionable neighbours.

The Victorian/Edwardian era

Conservative late-Victorian and Edwardian gentlemen golfers wore longer trousers with morning jackets and silk ties. Those longer trousers were known as 'plus twos' if they came two inches below the knee, or 'plus fours' if they dropped an even more sensible four inches. Even 'plus sixes' and 'plus eights' were available to the more modest players of the age. Plus fours in particular were popularised after King Edward VII was seen wearing them and Americans, knowing that wearing plus fours was as close as they would ever get to having a royal family of their own, suddenly couldn't get enough of them.

Women golfers of the time had an ensemble that consisted of a blouse with sleeves so fitted that they constricted the flow of blood through the arms and a long, flowing skirt that was guaranteed to catch the club head on the downswing.

Fore!

A totally pants idea!

In a last-ditch attempt to establish an American monarchy (see above), golfer Payne Stewart tried to bring back the plus-four style in the 1980s and 1990s, but he was met with a resounding 'No, you carry on, mate' from his fellow professionals.

Between the wars

The 1933 US Open in particular was something of a watershed moment for golfing attire, because it was played in a heatwave at a time when players were still dressed primarily to keep out the cold. Golfers started to experiment more and long-sleeved shirts started to take over from suit jackets. Bow ties became something of a feature at this time, being more practical than a hanging tie, as did the two-tone 'spectator shoes' so beloved of gangsters and Fred Astaire. Flannels became the order of the day as far as the bottom half was concerned, preferably plain white or grey, so that a chap could go straight from the office to the course.

For the ladies, knitted twin sets had become de rigueur and worked perfectly well except in heavy rain, when they probably weighed twice as much at the end of the round as they had on the first tee.

The pop and rock era

As new synthetic materials became available from the 1950s onwards, khaki trousers and polo shirts became staple golf wear. Smart-casual had arrived to stay. The women's practical 'skort'(a skirt with built-in shorts) arrived to finally combine freedom of movement with a degree of modesty. Clothing became ever more practical, with shoes spiked for improved traction and golf gloves becoming ubiquitous for better grip.

As pop turned to rock in the 1970s and 1980s, so beige and khaki turned to heavy patterns, outrageous checks and mad colours. Who knew that bright pink socks could go so well with green checked trousers and a fluorescent orange jumper? Only golfers, actually.

Fore!

The cutting edge of fashion

If you wanted to stand out as a professional golfer in the 1980s or 1990s, you had to wear a stylish polo shirt with a great white shark embroidered on it, a black straw hat with a great white shark embroidered on it, and a golf glove with a great white shark embroidered on it. If you could manage six feet of height, bleach your hair in the sun and get yourself a bit of a tan, so much the better. But just to be absolutely sure, you probably had to be Australian legend Greg Norman.

Late twentieth century

Golf shoes got non-metal studs instead of metal spikes for improved comfort and less damage to greens and locker-room floors, and golf clothes became increasingly comfortable, breathable and weatherproof. A moisture-eliminating, body-temperature-regulating base layer under a thermally insulated odour-eliminating mid layer covered with a well-ventilated weather-protective top layer left heavy wool a distant memory. As women's golf became increasingly popular, the same high standards now applied to their own versatile, practical clothing ranges.

Fore!

You've got to be joking, son

Swedish golfer Jesper Parnevik was the son of a top Swedish comedian, and it showed. During his Norman Wisdom phase (do a quick Internet search if you're too young to know) he wore an upturned peak on his baseball cap – when he played in the Ryder Cup, he even received a customised cap so that the Team Europe logo could be seen on the underside of his peak. During his disco phase, he wore purple trousers and a pork pie hat. He had many other phases, including his brief 'I'm wearing a necktie under my vest today' phase, and was even known to change his outfit in the middle of a round when the mood took him.

Twenty-first century

Now we're really talking, as manufacturers combine elegant designer style with athletic practicality. Today's clothes are guaranteed to knock several strokes off your handicap and you should think nothing of paying several hundred pounds, or dollars, for trousers that allow you to swing freely, or a pair of performance hybrid shoes made from Tibetan yak leather – scientists will have scanned the feet of thousands of athletes to ensure an exceptionally lightweight shoe that guarantees stability, allows you to feel the ground like never before, and maximises your swing power. Nothing can go wrong in these shoes.

Smart polo shirts remain the order of the day, unless you're too big a draw to bother about the etiquette of golfing fashion, e.g. if you're Tiger Woods, in which case you can just wear a T-shirt, but only if the sponsors' logos remain clearly visible at all times.

Fore!

Colourful character

Never a difficult man to pick out on a golf course himself (witness his combination of Union Jack vest and tartan trousers at the 2009 Open Championship), top English player Ian Poulter was so fed up with what he considered to be the bland and boring range of available golf wear, that he now designs his own 'funky' range. In a tip to the origins of the game, different-coloured tartans are a speciality.

CHAPTER 5

IN THE CLUB

I need a doctor. Ring the nearest golf club.
GROUCHO MARX, AMERICAN COMEDIAN AND ACTOR

The world of club golf

Far removed from the world of professional golf, which we will come to, players of all standards get together at their local golf clubs (or with their local golfing societies) around the world. There are tens of thousands of golf clubs across the globe, from northern Norway to southern Argentina, from Mount Kenya to the Great Australian Bight. In fact, the game has become so popular that its reach now extends to some unusual global extremities and into a lot of nooks and crannies in between. Here are my top ten golf clubs to literally go out of your way to play before you die:

Tromsø Golf Club
Norway

**Mount Kenya
Safari Club**
Nanyuki, Kenya

Coeur d'Alene Resort
Idaho, USA

La Paz Golf Club
Bolivia

Lost City Golf Cours
Sun City, South Africa

Ushuaia Golf Club
Argentina

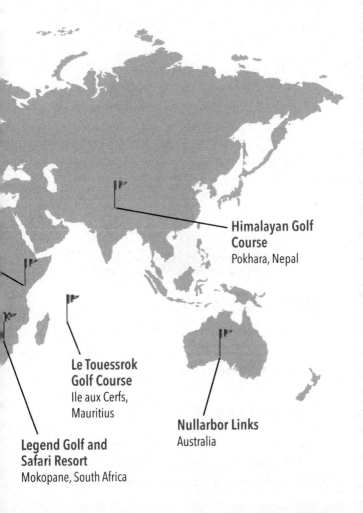

Himalayan Golf Course
Pokhara, Nepal

Le Touessrok Golf Course
Ile aux Cerfs,
Mauritius

Nullarbor Links
Australia

Legend Golf and Safari Resort
Mokopane, South Africa

Tromsø Golf Club, Norway

The most northerly golf course in the world, some 200 miles inside the Arctic Circle. Playable from May to October and remains open 24 hours a day during the period of the midnight sun.

Ushuaia Golf Club, Argentina

The most southerly golf course in the world, surrounded by the Patagonian Andes on Tierra del Fuego, just above Cape Horn. Playable from September to April.

Mount Kenya Safari Club, Nanyuki, Kenya

A nine-hole course that straddles both hemispheres. Cross the equator from north to south playing the seventh hole, and cross back into the northern hemisphere in time for gin o'clock on the verandah.

Nullarbor Links, Australia

More of a concept than a golf club, but nonetheless the longest golf course in the world, spanning 848 miles (1,365 kilometres)! Includes 11 desert holes constructed at 11 different roadhouses along the Eyre Highway across the Nullarbor Plain at the head of the Great Australian Bight. Average distance between holes is 41 miles (66 kilometres).

Lost City Golf Course, Sun City, South Africa

Sits amidst lush greenery in an otherwise semi-arid Bushveld environment. Best known for the 2-metre-long Nile crocodiles that guard the par-three 13th hole. Important to leave your next-of-kin details at the clubhouse.

Legend Golf and Safari Resort, Mokopane, South Africa

Each hole is designed by a different golfing legend and the additional 19th hole is probably the most challenging par-three in the world. The tee box, perched on the edge of Hanglip Mountain, is reached by helicopter, and the green is set in the shape of Africa 400 metres below.

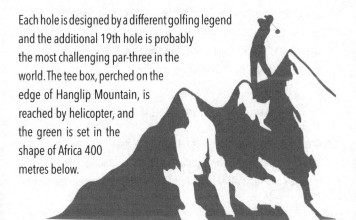

La Paz Golf Club, Bolivia

At 10,800 feet (3,290 metres) up in the Andes, the highest golf club in the world will leave you breathless, but at least the ball flies further at that altitude. Thanks to the local microclimate, the course is playable all year round in spring temperatures.

Coeur d'Alene Resort, Idaho, USA

Tucked away in the Rocky Mountains, the par-three 14th varies in length according to the positioning of the floating-island green. The Putter Boat Shuttle, made of Honduran mahogany, takes you across the scenic lake to hole out.

Himalayan Golf Course, Pokhara, Nepal

The clubhouse looks down over the canyon that contains the golf course, as do the many eagles that live on the canyon walls. The soundtrack of waterfalls and a bubbling snow-fed river will ensure Nirvana long before you finish your round.

Le Touessrok Golf Course, Ile aux Cerfs, Mauritius

A ten-minute boat ride from the resort itself, this tropical-island course is as close to earthly paradise as you're going to get. The views include coral reefs all around and a volcanic mountain on the skyline.

Clubbing together

Those who compete for their local club championship, or win their club's monthly medal, play a somewhat different game to those humble club golfers who live for the odd great shot. But they can all nonetheless compete together in a way not possible in most sports thanks to an age-old handicapping system designed to create a relatively level playing field across ability levels, and which today remains the most discussed topic in the 19th holes of golf clubs around the world. Every club and society has its 'bandits', those who are ribbed mercilessly for daring to play better than their handicap suggested they might.

When is a handicap not a handicap?

When it's a golfing handicap, basically. This is because players who are less competent are afforded the greatest assistance – for example, a 24-handicapper shooting a gross score of 94 will record a net score of 70, as will a 12-handicapper who has shot a gross score of 82.

Although handicaps are assessed on a player's previous scores against the par of a given course, they are primarily designed to reflect a player's potential. Players with higher handicaps are less likely to realise their potential on a regular basis, because they don't have the consistency of the lower handicappers. They are, therefore, more prone to have 'good days' and 'bad days'. Amateur-level and professional players do not have handicaps because they compete on level terms without them.

In addition to the basic handicapping system, a number of different types of competition have been devised to keep the game as competitive and as interesting as possible for as many golfers as possible, the two most common ones being Stableford and Texas Scramble.

Fore!

Stableford and Texas Scramble

Introduced by British army surgeon Dr Frank Stableford in the 1930s, Stableford is a system which awards points on each hole once an allowance has been made for a player's handicap. One advantage of this format is that players can recover from bad holes by playing better on later ones (but play enough holes badly and not even the good doctor will save you).

Texas Scramble is a fun team event that became popular as a means of cheering Texans up during the Great Depression. All members of the team tee off and then pick the best finishing position to determine the spot from which all team members will play the next shot, and so on, to the final putt of the hole. Scores are often unusually good because, for example, the fourth player to take a birdie putt has already seen the line and distance of the team's previous three attempts at the hole.

One big happy family?

It is no secret that golf was not always the inclusive sport that it now largely is, and would-be golfers often found themselves on the outside looking in because they were not of the right profession or social standing, or because they were not quite male enough or not quite white enough to be allowed in. These are increasingly issues of the past, not just because golf clubs can no longer afford to be fussy about whose money they take, but also because the breaking down of social barriers within golf clubs has largely kept in step with that of society generally.

Even Augusta National finally started to fall into line when it admitted its first two female members in 2012, one of whom was none other than Condoleezza Rice, the former US Secretary of State, who thereby became Augusta's first black female member – a politically correct appointment, if ever there was one. But some male bastions are hanging in there, including four Open Championship venues, and Clare Balding famously refused to cover the Open Championship at Muirfield in 2013 for the BBC on the grounds that she could never become a member there.

More and more clubs, though, can be seen relaxing their membership policies and fewer and fewer of them do not include a family membership amongst their offerings. Dress codes – which at some clubs are overtly strict – have also become more relaxed and I have even seen some younger chaps playing with their polo shirts *outside their trousers*, no names mentioned. (It was Greg and Keith Wapling.)

Fore!

Political big hitters (and a king)

Many golf clubs can boast famous members, past or present, but few can boast four different British prime ministers and a short-lived king. Walton Heath Golf Club in Surrey can. Arthur Balfour, David Lloyd George, Andrew Bonar Law and Winston Churchill all graced its fairways and drank its brandy, and Edward, Prince of Wales, was its first captain in 1935, before briefly becoming King Edward VIII the following year.

And now for something completely different

If standard golf clubs and competitions are not your thing and you are looking for something a bit more unconventional, there are some quirky societies and tournaments that might just fit the bill:

Hickory societies

If time travel is your thing, you might want to join one of the increasing number of 'societies of hickory golfers', whose members are keen to preserve the early traditions of the game by using pre-1935 hickory-shafted clubs and turning out in plus fours. There are national championships around the world that lead to the best individual players (men and women) and international teams being invited to compete in the World Hickory Open Golf Championship, held each year on one of the famous Scottish traditional links courses. If you don't want to take it that seriously, you can just play hickory golf for fun, and you can even hire hickory clubs to play on the oldest surviving golf course in the world at Musselburgh Links, near Edinburgh.

Snow (or ice) golf

English writer Rudyard Kipling was one of the first proponents of snow golf, playing with red balls during breaks from writing *The Jungle Book* in wintery 1890s Vermont. The World Ice Golf Championship is held annually on a course laid out on the shifting icebergs of Uummannaq, Greenland. The course is finalised just a few days before the start of the championship, to ensure it is still there when the tournament gets underway. Greens are white (and slippy) and balls are fluorescent orange.

Nude golf

For those who enjoy swinging freely, La Jenny Naturist Resort and Golf Club near Bordeaux in south-west France was opened in 1993 to cater specifically for *au naturel* golfers.

Speed golf

Also known to its proponents around the world as 'hit and run' golf, the main difference between this and standard golf is that players wear trainers to run between shots. Scoring involves adding the number of strokes taken to the time taken to get round the course, so a round of 80 in 59 minutes is a score of 139. The Guinness World Record stands at 109:06, a round of 65 in 44:06, shot by American Christopher Smith carrying just six clubs.

Disc golf

Dispense with clubs and balls altogether and try your hand with a Frisbee. Played in over 40 countries on purpose-built courses, players use different discs for tee shots, mid-range shots and 'putting', which involves flying the Frisbee into a basket or onto a flat target. Throws that need to be mastered include the 'hatchet', the 'grenade' and the 'chicken wing'.

Night golf

For golfers with not enough time in the day, night golf involves hitting luminous balls along barely lit fairways (which look like airport runways). Flags and hazards are also illuminated, but judging distance is particularly challenging when the usual landmarks are nowhere to be seen. If it all proves too difficult, try the fully lit Faldo Course in Dubai, instigated to avoid expats having to play in the searing heat of the desert day.

The Bobby Jones Open

Every year since 1979 Bob Joneses from around the world have come together on a US course to play a tournament in honour of the great golfer. There is a growing concern, however, that not enough Mr and Mrs Joneses are naming their sons Robert, so a campaign is underway to encourage more of them to do so for the long-term sake of the tournament.

The club professional

What this means depends very much on which club working professionals find themselves at. At a club or resort with a number of courses, they may be elevated in title to Director of Golf. If they are at a club mainly to give golf lessons, they may be referred to as the teaching professional or golf coach. If they are at a small to medium-sized club, they probably give lessons, run the golf shop, take the green fees and do anything else that needs doing to make sure the club runs smoothly.

If they make it to the big time as a professional golfer, though, they can forget about all that stuff, because touring professionals are too busy playing golf to be getting their hands dirty. Rory McIlroy is the touring professional at Lough Erne Resort in Northern Ireland, but he's unlikely to be there when you want some help with your chipping, or when you want to buy a Mars Bar and a Gatorade to keep you going at the turn.

CHAPTER 6

THE AMATEUR GAME

Golf is a game that is played on a five-inch course – the distance between your ears.

BOBBY JONES, THE MOST SUCCESSFUL AMATEUR GOLFER IN HISTORY

Introduction

In Britain, the secretary of Royal Liverpool Golf Club inaugurated the Amateur Championship in 1885 and it remains today the most important amateur event in the R & A's calendar. Many past winners have gone on to have successful professional careers, including Spaniards José María Olazábal and Sergio García. Some of the great amateur winners, however, chose to remain amateur golfers throughout their careers, including Englishmen John Ball and Michael Bonallack (see below).

The US Amateur was first played in 1895 and its past winners include American golfing legends Bobby Jones, Arnold Palmer, Jack Nicklaus, Phil Mickelson and Tiger Woods.

Both the Amateur Championship and the US Amateur were designated majors before professional golf became dominant in the mid twentieth century, so it is perhaps appropriate that the winners of the amateur championships today are granted automatic entry to the next Open Championship, Masters and US Open.

Amateur Championship – most wins

8	John Ball	England	1888, 1890, 1892, 1894, 1899, 1907, 1910, 1912
5	Michael Bonallack	England	1961, 1965, 1968, 1969, 1970
4	Harold Hilton	England	1900, 1901, 1911, 1913
3	Joe Carr	Ireland	1953, 1958, 1960

Note: Michael Bonallack went on to become secretary of the R & A from 1984 to 1999.

US Amateur – most wins

5	Bobby Jones	USA	1924, 1925, 1927, 1928, 1930
4	Jerome Travers	USA	1907, 1908, 1912, 1913
3	Walter Travis	USA	1900, 1901, 1903
3	Tiger Woods	USA	1994, 1995, 1996

'Low amateur'

Open Championship

Since 1949 the Silver Medal has been awarded to the amateur with the lowest score, and therefore the highest finishing position, in the Open Championship. Young winners who have gone on to big things on the professional circuit once they started shaving include Hal Sutton (USA), José María Olazábal (Spain), Tiger Woods (USA), Justin Rose (England) and Rory McIlroy (Northern Ireland).

US Open

Bobby Jones was US Open 'low amateur' on no fewer than ten occasions. In 1960, a fresh-faced Jack Nicklaus posted the lowest ever score in the tournament by an amateur, when he finished second overall, just two strokes behind Arnold Palmer.

Masters

Since 1952, the Silver Cup has been awarded to the amateur with the highest finishing position in the Masters. Jack Nicklaus (USA), Ben Crenshaw (USA), Phil Mickelson (USA), Tiger Woods (USA), Sergio García (Spain) and Hunter Mahan (USA) are all top golfers who won the trophy while still wet behind the ears. In 2013, it was won by an even wetter-eared competitor, 14-year-old Chinese schoolboy Guan Tianlang, who probably had some homework to catch up on the following week!

PGA Championship

The only major that no amateurs are invited to compete in.

Robert Tyre Jones

American Bobby Jones only ever turned professional as a lawyer, but he managed to find time in between briefs to become the best amateur player in the history of the game. Playing only part-time, essentially for three months each summer, he remains the only golfer in history, amateur or professional, to have won the Grand Slam, which in pre-Masters 1930 constituted the Open and Amateur Championships of Britain and America. He won 13 majors in all, including three Open Championships and four US Opens, between 1923 and 1930. He then retired from playing the game at the age of just 28 in order to find time to pursue some other interests, like designing the Augusta National course and co-founding the Masters tournament. For an amateur, Bobby Jones was anything but.

Walker Cup

The Walker Cup is a biennial match-play team event between the amateur golfers of the USA and Great Britain & Ireland. It is named after George Walker (the grandfather of George Bush, Snr), who donated the first trophy in 1922. The USA have dominated the competition, winning the first nine competitions played and leading 35–8 overall, but the teams have been more evenly matched in recent times, with five wins apiece in the last ten competitions. Bobby Jones won all five of the singles matches he played for the USA, and Englishman Luke Donald won all four of his for Great Britain & Ireland before turning professional.

Curtis Cup

The Curtis Cup is the equivalent of the Walker Cup for amateur women golfers. First played at Wentworth in 1932, it is named after sisters Harriot and Margaret Curtis, the leading American amateur players who donated the trophy. The Americans have dominated the competition and the overall score stands at 27–7. In 2004, 14-year-old American child prodigy Michelle Wie became the youngest ever player in the competition, winning both her singles matches into the bargain. In 2008, American Stacy Lewis made history by winning all five of her matches (one singles, two foursomes and two fourballs).

THE PROFESSIONAL GAME

If you wish to hide your character, do not play golf.
Ian Poulter, English Ryder Cup hero

The tough get going

Golf today is played around the world at the very highest levels of sporting achievement. The professionals hit golf balls over unfeasibly long distances (regularly driving the ball over 300 yards), and for the most part combine their huge power with impressive accuracy. They add wizardry of Harry Potter-esque proportions when they get anywhere near the putting surface, where touch and feel suddenly matter more than raw power. But even that combination is not enough to take the huge prizes and the glory that await those who reach the very pinnacles of the game. For that you have to add the mental toughness required to perform under severe pressure over four consecutive days in a very public arena. Professional golf is not a game for the faint-hearted.

However good the professionals get, though, they cannot play every shot perfectly; they cannot break par on every hole; they cannot win every tournament they enter. The very greatest players of the game have therefore had to learn to cope with disappointment, with failure, with missed opportunity, and with the very visible humiliation that comes with messing up when a trophy had been there for the taking only moments before.

For those that stay 'in the zone' the longest, and bounce back from disappointment the quickest, untold riches and worldwide fame await.

The Golden Bear and the Tiger

Many people think that if Tiger Woods gets his act together again in terms of winning majors (a long drought began after the US Open in 2008), he can still go on to get the five he needs to surpass Jack Nicklaus's record of 18 and thereby become the greatest golfer to have ever lived. Others believe that the greatest golfer to have ever lived needs to have won the most major championships and needs also to have been the best ambassador the game has ever had. If we bring charisma and humility into the equation, Tiger Woods will arguably never surpass Jack Nicklaus as the greatest golfer the world has ever seen.

Top gun

Arguments have raged since competitive golf began about who the best golfer has been of a particular generation, and even about who has been the best golfer of all time. Some have put forward a case for the best golfer in history being the player who has spent the most time as the world's number one ranked golfer (Tiger Woods); some have argued that it should be the player who has won the most tour events irrespective of whether these events were major championships (American legend Sam Snead); but most long-time observers of the game reckon that it's about winning the majors, and no one has won more than Jack Nicklaus (18).

A world sport

Following a period of early Scottish domination (admittedly much of it taking place before many other countries started taking the game seriously), American players came to dominate the professional game from the 1910s onwards. There were always some notable exceptions from Europe and the southern hemisphere, but it is only in recent times that non-Americans have started to take a more meaningful share of the major trophies. Of the 427 majors played between the first Open Championship in 1860 and the PGA Championship in 2013, 262 were won by Americans, 114 by Europeans and 51 by players from the rest of the world.

The fairy tale of the early 2010s has been the extent to which the small country of Northern Ireland has punched above its weight on the world stage, with three separate major winners in a two-year period. As golf has spread around the globe in recent times, more and more countries have produced a share of the game's top players. The following list of countries that have produced major-championship winners (with the number of majors won in parentheses) will prove the point:

Scotland (55)

Northern Ireland (5)

Ireland (3)

Canada (1)

Wales (1)

Jersey (9)

France (1)

Spain (7)

USA (262)

Argentina (3)

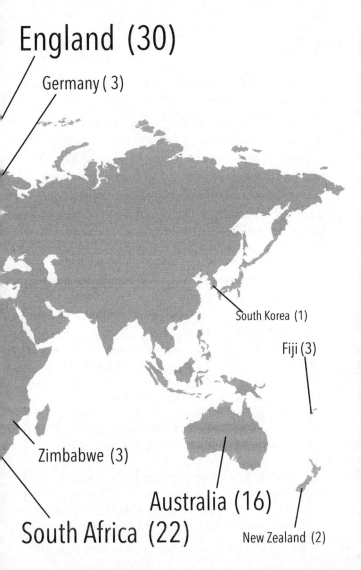

England (30)

Germany (3)

South Korea (1)

Fiji (3)

Zimbabwe (3)

Australia (16)

South Africa (22)

New Zealand (2)

Go Jersey!

Yes, you read that correctly. The Bailiwick of Jersey has produced more major winners than Spain. This is mainly thanks to the great Harry Vardon, who still holds the record of six Open Championship wins (plus a US Open for good measure), and who remains further immortalised by the 'Vardon grip', the overlapping method by which most golfers today still stop the club from flying out of their hands. Ted Ray, who grew up on the same island idolising Vardon at the turn of the twentieth century, went on to add an Open Championship and a US Open of his own.

Fore!

So near and yet, so far

The list of great golfers who have never lifted a major trophy is a long one, and at the time of writing includes Luke Donald (England), Sergio García (Spain), Dustin Johnson (USA), Lee Westwood (England), Colin Montgomerie (Scotland), Steve Stricker (USA), Matt Kuchar (USA) and Ian Poulter (England). Phil Mickelson spent a long time on that list but dropped off it when he finally started to win major trophies in 2004. He is still the holder of another record that no one wants, though, and it is one which will probably never be beaten: he has spent 270 weeks ranked number two in the world, without ever making it to number one.

Great rivalries

Great sport throws up great rivalries. Sometimes this has the effect of two or more players spurring each other on to ever-greater achievements. At other times a player breaks under the pressure of it all and is left wondering what they might have achieved if only their great rival hadn't been around to spoil things. Let's have a look at some of the greats who happened to bump into each other on the same golf courses at the same time:

The three triumvirates

The so-called Great Triumvirate comprised the three leading golfers of the late nineteenth and early twentieth centuries: Harry Vardon (Jersey), John Henry Taylor (England) and James Braid (Scotland), who together won the Open Championship 16 times.

The first American triumvirate of Bobby Jones, Gene Sarazen and Walter Hagen took 25 majors together between 1914 and 1935 and their hard-fought battles during the 1920s in particular captured the public's imagination around the world.

The second American triumvirate of Sam Snead, Byron Nelson and Ben Hogan rescued golf from the depths of the Great Depression and gave desperate Americans in particular something to cheer about with their flamboyant success. Together, between 1937 and 1954, they won 21 majors.

The Big Three

The first modern triumvirate was too modern to be called a triumvirate, so it was known instead as 'The Big Three'. Ferocious rivals but lifelong friends, Arnold Palmer, Jack Nicklaus and Gary Player thrilled galleries around the world whenever and wherever they pitted their skills against each other. The fact that Player was South African added a thrilling new dimension as the greatness of the game and its top players became increasingly international. Together the trio were a formidable force for a period in the 1960s, but their major-winning careers didn't overlap for long because Nicklaus inevitably had to march on without the other two in his successful quest to become the best golfer of all time.

The Big Five

Born within 12 months of one another in five different countries in 1957/1958, the Big Five of Seve Ballesteros (Spain), Nick Faldo (England), Bernhard Langer (Germany), Sandy Lyle (Scotland) and Ian Woosnam (Wales) took European golf to unprecedented heights in the modern era. Together, they won 16 majors between 1979 and 1996, and they also helped to transform the Europeans into a Ryder Cup force capable of competing on equal terms with the USA.

The great duels

Probably the most thrilling mano-a-mano contests to watch were between Jack Nicklaus and fellow American Tom Watson. The pair slugged it out in their 'Duel in the Sun' for the Open Championship at Turnberry in 1977, when Watson ultimately won by one stroke, and in the climax of the US Open in 1982 at Pebble Beach, when Watson came up with 'that chip' from thick grass on the 71st hole for the first of two closing birdies that would again pip the mighty Nicklaus at the post.

And probably the most uncomfortable duel to watch was the one where Nick Faldo destroyed Greg Norman in the last round of the 1996 Masters at Augusta National. The world squirmed as Faldo held his nerve and Norman visibly lost his, throwing away a six-shot lead at the start of play to lose by five.

Beasts of burden

Let us not forget the magnificent beasts of burden who do the really hard work on the course – the caddies. As we have seen, caddies pre-dated golf bags and spent the eighteenth century carrying clubs loose in their hands. When the first canvas 'pencil bags' arrived at the turn of the twentieth century, they were lightweight affairs compared to the heavy equipment that needs to be heaved around the course today.

But caddies today are much more than heavy lifters. They also advise on shot distance, wind direction, club selection, the line and weight of the putt, and even the tactics to employ depending on the state of the leaderboard. They provide moral support and the right amount of encouragement at the right time.

And long gone are the days when they did the job for tips. At the top level of the professional game, caddies can earn half a million dollars (around £300,000) a year plus the expenses required to accompany their players around the world. Some stay with their players for many a year, some even become lifelong friends. And some have become famous in their own right:

Steve Williams

The New Zealander is best known for caddying for Tiger Woods from 1999 to 2011, during which time he is reputed to have earned $12 million (£7.2 million), but before that he had worked for some other great players including Australians Peter Thomson and Greg Norman and American Ray Floyd. After parting company with Tiger, he teamed up with top Australian player, Adam Scott.

His most embarrassing moment probably came at the 2006 Ryder Cup at the K Club in Ireland. He slipped while cleaning Woods's 9-iron at the seventh hole and dropped it into deep water. The club was later retrieved by a diver and returned to Williams on the 15th hole.

Fanny Sunesson

The Swede has worked for Fred Funk (USA), Henrik Stenson (Sweden) and Sergio García, but she really became a household name when caddying for Nick Faldo during his major-winning years. She is now a full-time coach and golf adviser, including being mental coach to the top German golfer Martin Kaymer.

Jim 'Bones' Mackay

The only caddie Phil Mickelson has ever won a professional tournament with. Mackay previously carried for Americans Larry Mize, Scott Simpson and Curtis Strange, but it was fellow American Fred Couples who gave the lanky six-foot-four-inch caddy his nickname after he couldn't remember his real name.

Alfie Fyles

The Englishman caddied for Tom Watson on each of his five Open Championship wins.

Bruce Edwards

Tom Watson's caddie back home in America for almost 30 years. His life is chronicled in John Feinstein's 2005 book *Caddy For Life: The Bruce Edwards Story*.

Nathan 'Iron Man' Avery

Before 1983, Augusta National required white-only players to use local, black-only caddies. Arnold Palmer used Iron Man's local knowledge to good effect in winning four Masters titles.

Jack Nicklaus II

Caddied for the best golfer of all time, his father, when Jack I triumphed one last time in the Masters at Augusta in 1986.

Fore!

We've got them licked, Francis!

One player–caddie image even made it onto a US postage stamp in 1988. The image was of the pint-sized ten-year-old Eddie Lowery caddying for the 20-year-old American Francis Ouimet on his way to victory in the 1913 US Open at Brookline, Massachusetts. The unlikely partnership and Ouimet's unlikely victory that year have also been immortalised in Mark Frost's 2002 book The Greatest Game Ever Played, *and a film adaptation followed in 2005 (see chapter headed 'Golf on Film').*

Global structure

Professional golf is a worldwide sport, and a worldwide sport needs a worldwide structure. Golf has exactly that, and it includes the following worthy bodies:

R & A
International Federation of PGA Tours
PGA Tour (USA, Canada and Latin America)
PGA of America
PGA European Tour
Japan Golf Tour
PGA Tour of Australasia
Sunshine Tour (Southern Africa)
Asian Tour (except Japan)

The role played by each of those bodies is as follows:

The R & A

The R & A sanctions the rules of golf and administers a number of tournaments and international matches, including the Open Championship (see next chapter), the oldest and most important major championship in golf.

International Federation of PGA Tours

Formed in 1996 as an umbrella organisation to coordinate common or global issues that affect different tours around the world. The Federation sanctions the Official World Golf Ranking and in 1999 founded the World Golf Championships, a group of four annual events considered by many to be second in importance only to the four major championships.

PGA Tour (USA, Canada and Latin America)

The PGA Tour runs most events week-to-week throughout the year, mostly in the USA, but also in Canada and Latin America. Its signature event is the Players Championship, the so-called 'fifth major' that is held each year at the TPC course at Sawgrass in Florida.

It also administers the FedEx Cup, a fairly convoluted points system that has replaced the previous more straightforward money-winners list. The PGA Tour also administers the Presidents Cup, a biennial Ryder Cup-style competition between the USA and the Rest of the World, and the Champions Tour for professional golfers who have reached the age of 50.

Fore!

Put out to (luscious) grass

Previously known as the Senior Tour, it was presumably renamed the Champions Tour to let senior players feel less senior and more champion. Golf is unique among sports in having high-profile and lucrative competitions for players of this age group. Nearly all of the famous golfers who are eligible to compete in these events choose to do so, and a number of these senior (I mean 'champion') players win over a million dollars (£600,000) in prize money each season. Once endorsements and other business activities are taken into account, a few of the legends of golf in this age group can earn as much as the younger PGA Tour professionals. Enough to cover the hip replacements, certainly.

PGA of America

The association that represents club professionals throughout America and which administers the PGA Championship major tournament and, in conjunction with the PGA European Tour, the Ryder Cup.

PGA European Tour

The European Tour used to be regarded as something of a feeder system for the PGA Tour in America, but it has been going increasingly global in its own right in recent years, in part by holding events outside Europe, e.g. in Tunisia, Dubai and Thailand. In parallel with the similar development in America, the previously simple Order of Merit has been replaced by a more complicated points system known as the Race to Dubai, which culminates in the top-ranked players being invited to play in the money-spinning finale to the season, the DP World Tour Championship in Dubai.

In conjunction with the PGA of America, the PGA European Tour also administers the biennial Ryder Cup between Europe and the USA.

Japan Golf Tour

Founded in 1973, its most successful 'exports' to the PGA Tour have been Isao Aoki (World Match Play Champion in 1978 and US Open runner-up in 1980) and Masashi 'Jumbo' Ozaki (often in the world's top ten in the 1990s).

PGA Tour of Australasia

Sanctions events held in Australia, New Zealand and Fiji. Its Order of Merit winners have included major-championship winners Greg Norman, Geoff Ogilvy and Adam Scott.

Sunshine Tour (Southern Africa)

Previously known as the South African Tour, it rebranded itself in 2000 in the hope of broadening its appeal. It sanctions events in South Africa, Namibia, Swaziland, Zambia and Zimbabwe. Only open to non-white players since 1991, the Tour's most successful 'exports' have included South Africans Gary Player, Ernie Els, Trevor Immelman and Charles Schwartzel, and Zimbabweans Mark McNulty and Nick Price.

Asian Tour (except Japan)

Sanctions events in Brunei, Cambodia, Hong Kong, India, Indonesia, Malaysia, Myanmar (Burma), Singapore, South Korea, Taiwan, Thailand and the Philippines. Thai golfers have been most successful, so it was something of a surprise when England's Simon Dyson won the Asian Order of Merit in 2000. Having just turned professional, and having failed to secure a card to play on the European Tour, Dyson tried his luck in Asia and won three tournaments to top the Asian money list before joining the European Tour the following year.

CHAPTER 8

THE
MAJORS

You don't feather shots on the last hole of a major championship.

Jack Nicklaus, American golfing legend

The four majors – an introduction

There are four 'major' tournaments each year: the original Open Championship in Britain, plus three others in America. They are always held in the same chronological order:

Masters (April)
US Open (June)
Open Championship (July)
PGA Championship (August)

The immortals

Winning one major championship brings fame and fortune. Winning several brings golfing immortality. Here is the list of the all-time greats who have won the most major championships as at the end of 2013:

Steve Ballesteros

Spain

5

James Braid

Scotland

5

John Henry Taylor

England

5

Gary Player

South Africa

9

Tiger Woods

USA

14

Peter Thompson

Australia

5

Walter Hagan

USA

11

Gene Sarazen

USA

7

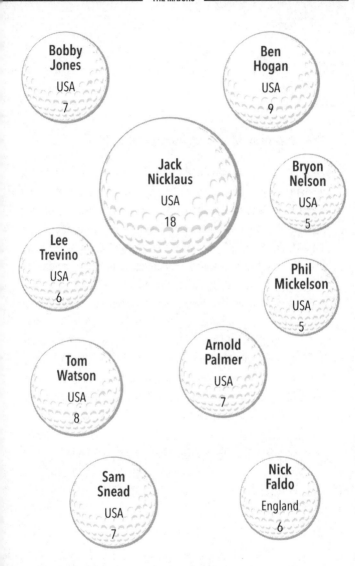

Bobby
Jones
USA
7

Ben
Hogan
USA
9

Jack
Nicklaus
USA
18

Bryon
Nelson
USA
5

Lee
Trevino
USA
6

Phil
Mickelson
USA
5

Tom
Watson
USA
8

Arnold
Palmer
USA
7

Sam
Snead
USA
7

Nick
Faldo
England
6

The 'impregnable quadrilateral' of golf

Winning all four majors in the same year would constitute the modern golfing Grand Slam, as determined by Arnold Palmer in a plane on the way to Scotland for the 1960 Open Championship at St Andrews. His aim was to recreate the modern equivalent of Bobby Jones' Grand Slam in 1930, when the *New York Sun* wrote that Jones had achieved the 'impregnable quadrilateral of golf', whereas the *Atlanta Journal* dubbed it (the less-of-a-mouthful) 'Grand Slam'.

The modern Grand Slam has never been achieved, but Tiger Woods has achieved the next best thing, the Consecutive Grand Slam, after winning the US Open, Open Championship and PGA Championship in 2000, followed immediately by the Masters in 2001. Only four other golfers have achieved the next best thing again, the Career Grand Slam, which means winning each major at least once in your career: Gene Sarazen, Ben Hogan, Gary Player and Jack Nicklaus.

This chapter now looks at each of the four majors in turn.

Masters

Prize fund: *c.* $8 million
(£4.8 million)

Winner's purse: *c.* $1.5
million (£900,000)

Trophy: Masters Trophy

Other spoils of victory:

Ceremonial green jacket,
gold medal

Introduction

Played since 1934, the Masters is always the first major championship of the year, finishing on the second Sunday in April. It is always held at Augusta National in Georgia – the only major that is always played on the same course.

The winner is presented with the ceremonial green jacket in the Butler Cabin soon after the end of the tournament, and shortly thereafter with a gold medal and a sterling silver replica of the Masters trophy, which depicts the Augusta National clubhouse.

The Augusta National course

Co-designed by Bobby Jones, Augusta National opened in 1933 on the site of a former indigo plantation, and a quick glance at the Augusta scorecard tells you that the scenery isn't going to be drab. Starting on 'Tea Olive', competitors play appropriately named holes like 'Pink Dogwood', 'Flowering Peach', 'Magnolia', 'Carolina Cherry', 'White Dogwood', 'Azalea' and 'Chinese Fir' before finally arriving in a meditative state at the eighteenth green on 'Holly'.

But all that beauty comes at a price, because the players will face few tougher challenges than Augusta the whole year through. They will have to contend with Amen Corner (a tough section running between the eleventh and thirteenth holes, with the notorious Rae's Creek never far away), lightning-fast greens (it is not uncommon for putts to roll past the hole, off the green and into a water hazard), and kiss-of-death shots over water towards the end of the round, by which time their nerves are shot to hell anyway (not many leaders at the start of the final day go on to win the tournament).

Fore!

A bunch of amateurs

Because the tournament was established by Bobby Jones, the most famous amateur golfer of all, the organisers always invite the most recent winners of the world's most prestigious amateur events to take part in the Masters. The reigning US Amateur champion always gets to play the first two rounds alongside the defending Masters champion, and every year the amateurs in the field even get to stay in the 'Crow's Nest' lodge at the top of the Augusta clubhouse.

Fore!

The demise of the Eisenhower Tree

One iconic Augusta hazard that stood tall for over a hundred years was the 65-foot (20-metre) loblolly pine in the seventeenth fairway that became known as the Eisenhower Tree. The former US president, a long-time member at Augusta, got so fed up hitting it with his tee shot that he suggested at a club meeting in 1956 that it be chopped down. Rather than refuse the request of the US president outright, the Augusta National chairman immediately adjourned the meeting to avoid taking a decision, but 'Ike' finally got his way in February 2014 when snow and ice caused so much damage that the tree had to be removed. Tiger Woods was probably more pleased than anyone – in 2011 he slipped on the pine straw while playing a shot from underneath the tree and damaged his left knee and Achilles tendon. Unable to play for the next four months, he quickly plummeted from number one to number fifty-eight in the world.

A potted history of the Masters

1934: The first tournament is won by American, Horton Smith.

1935: The Masters and the Augusta National course are propelled into public consciousness after Gene Sarazen plays 'the shot that was heard around the world', a three-wood into the hole for an albatross two at the par-five 15th hole on his way to winning the tournament.

1943–1945: World War Two stops play. Cattle and turkey are raised on the grounds to assist the war effort.

1949: A green jacket is awarded to the winner (Sam Snead) for the first time.

1961: South African Gary Player becomes the first non-American to win the Masters.

1966: Jack Nicklaus becomes the first player to successfully defend the trophy.

1975: Lee Elder becomes the first African American to play in the event.

1980: Seve Ballesteros becomes the first European to win the Masters.

1986: Jack Nicklaus becomes the oldest player to win the Masters (at 46 years of age). It is his sixth and last victory.

1987: Larry Mize chips in from 45 yards to win a play-off for the title from Greg Norman.

1988: Scotland's Sandy Lyle becomes the first British player to win the title, doing so with a miraculous 'up and down' from a fairway bunker at the final hole.

1996: England's Nick Faldo wins his third Masters after overhauling the six-stroke lead that Greg Norman had at the start of the final day.

1997: Tiger Woods becomes the youngest player to win the Masters (at the age of 21), and wins by a record margin of 12 strokes, and with a record low score of 18 under par.

2003: Mike Weir becomes the first left-hander (and the first Canadian) to win the tournament.

2011: South African Charl Schwartzel wins after making birdies on each of the last four holes.

2013: Adam Scott finally ends the long Australian wait for a Masters champion.

Most wins

6	Jack Nicklaus	USA	1963, 1965, 1966, 1972, 1975, 1986
4	Arnold Palmer	USA	1958, 1960, 1962, 1964
4	Tiger Woods	USA	1997, 2001, 2002, 2005
3	Jimmy Demaret	USA	1940, 1947, 1950
3	Sam Snead	USA	1949, 1952, 1954
3	Gary Player	South Africa	1961, 1974, 1978
3	Nick Faldo	England	1989, 1990, 1996
3	Phil Mickelson	USA	2004, 2006, 2010

Fore!

The curse of the par-three contest

The par-three contest that was introduced on Augusta's par-three course in 1960 takes place each year on the Wednesday preceding the tournament. It is huge fun for the spectators, with over 70 holes-in-one witnessed to date, i.e. more than one a year. Many players use family members and friends as caddies on the day, one of the most famous being Rory McIlroy's girlfriend in 2013, Danish former world number one tennis player, Caroline Wozniacki. The competition also serves as useful short-game practice for the players on the eve of the Masters tournament, but winning comes with a curse, since no winner of the par-three contest has ever gone on to be Masters champion in the same year.

Masters trivia

British golfers won four Masters titles in a row between 1988 and 1991: Sandy Lyle (1988); Nick Faldo (1989, 1990) and Ian Woosnam (1991).

Jack Nicklaus, Nick Faldo and Tiger Woods are the only three golfers to have successfully defended the Masters title the following year.

It is a requirement that all caddies wear the traditional white jumpsuit, green Masters cap and white trainers while on the course.

Zimbabwean Nick Price (in 1986) and Australian Greg Norman (in 1996) share the record low score of 63 in a Masters round. Nick Price likes to joke that his is better because he used a medieval (aka 'wooden') driver.

Argentinian Roberto de Vicenzo missed out on a play-off for the 1968 Masters because he failed to spot that his playing partner had put him down for a par four instead of the birdie three he actually scored on the 17th hole.

The 'pimento cheese sandwich' is to Masters' spectators what the hot dog is to baseball fans.

The Eisenhower Cabin is one of ten houses in the grounds of Augusta National available as lodgings to members. It was built in 1953 to Secret Service standards to house the president on his visits to the club (he had become a member in 1948).

Fore!

What's for dinner, champ?

The Champions Dinner held each year on the Tuesday preceding the tournament is always hosted (and paid for) by the defending champion, who also chooses the menu. Notable culinary choices have included Sandy Lyle's haggis, Nick Faldo's fish and chips and Mike Weir's elk, wild boar and Arctic char (that's a fish). After an Australian (Adam Scott) finally won the Masters in 2013, past champions spent the next year worrying that they might have to eat witchetty grubs, but probably not as much as they worried about eating Sandy Lyle's haggis. Bernhard Langer served up Wiener Schnitzel, obviously having forgotten momentarily that Vienna lies outside his home country of Germany.

US Open

Prize fund: *c.*$8 million
(£4.8 million)

Winner's purse: *c.*$1.5
million (£900,000)

Trophy: US Open
Championship Trophy

Other spoils of victory:

Gold medal

Introduction

The US Open is the second major of the year, finishing on the third Sunday in June, which happens to be Father's Day (so a golfing father is usually thanked profusely in the winner's acceptance speech). It is staged at a variety of clubs, always set up to make scoring so difficult that the tournament is often won at level par or higher. The most frequent venue has been Oakmont Country Club, Pennsylvania (eight times, which will become nine in 2016), followed by Baltusrol, New Jersey (seven) and Oakland Hills, Michigan (six).

A potted history of the US Open

1895: Englishman Horace Rawlins wins the first US Open, played in a single day over four rounds of a nine-hole course at Newport, Rhode Island.

1911: Nineteen-year-old American John McDermott finally produces a home-grown victory. He remains the youngest ever winner of the tournament.

1960: Arnold Palmer makes the greatest comeback in US Open history by overcoming the seven-stroke deficit he faced at the start of the final round. He wins by two strokes from a young amateur named Jack Nicklaus.

1965: South African Gary Player becomes the first winner from the southern hemisphere.

1990: American Hale Irwin becomes the oldest winner of the tournament (at 45 years of age).

2000: Tiger Woods wins by 15 strokes, the highest winning margin of any major championship to date.

2004–2007: A streak of four non-American wins occurs for the first time since 1910: Retief Goosen (South Africa); Michael Campbell (New Zealand); Geoff Ogilvy (Australia) and Angel Cabrera (Argentina).

2010: Northern Ireland's Graeme McDowell becomes the first European to win since Tony Jacklin in 1970.

2011: Rory McIlroy secures a second consecutive win for Northern Ireland and makes nonsense of the supposedly difficult set-up of US Open courses to win with a record score of 16 under par. Graeme McDowell had won at level par the previous year and the next two US Opens would be won at one over par.

2013: Justin Rose becomes the first English player to win since Tony Jacklin in 1970.

Most wins

4	Willie Anderson	Scotland	1901, 1903, 1904, 1905
4	Bobby Jones	USA	1923, 1926, 1929, 1930
4	Ben Hogan	USA	1948, 1950, 1951, 1953
4	Jack Nicklaus	USA	1962, 1967, 1972, 1980
3	Hale Irwin	USA	1974, 1979, 1990
3	Tiger Woods	USA	2000, 2002, 2008

US Open trivia

Scottish golfers emigrated en masse as club professionals to the States at the end of the nineteenth century and won 12 out of the first 16 US Opens.

Americans made the tournament their own from 1911 onwards (presumably as soon as they had finished taking lessons from the immigrant Scottish club professionals), with only nine non-American wins for the remainder of the century.

In a 65-year spell, between 1928 and 1993, only three non-Americans won the tournament: South African Gary Player (1965), Englishman Tony Jacklin (1970), and Australian David Graham (1981).

In a latter-day reversal of fortunes, Americans only won three times out of ten in the US Opens held between 2004 and 2013.

Rory McIlroy set 11 US Open records in a single tournament at Congressional Country Club in 2011, including lowest total score (268) and lowest total below par (at 16 under).

In 2012, Chinese amateur Andy Zhang, at the age of just 14, became the youngest player to compete in the tournament.

Phil Mickelson has finished runner-up six times at the US Open, the only major to have so far eluded him.

The set-up of the Pinehurst No. 2 course in 2005 was considered so tough that American former winner Johnny Miller described approach shots to the undulating greens as 'like trying to hit a ball on to the top of a VW Beetle'. A score of level par won the tournament.

The Open Championship

Prize fund: *c.*£5.5 million
($9.2 million)

Winner's purse: *c.*£1 million
($1.7 million)

Trophy: The Golf Champion
Trophy (aka the Claret Jug)

Other spoils of victory:

Gold medal

Introduction

The Open Championship is the third major of the year, taking place each July on one of a number of British links courses. The most frequent venue has been the Old Course at St Andrews (28 times), followed by Prestwick (24), Muirfield (16) and Royal St George's (14). It is the oldest major championship by some 35 years, having first taken place in 1860.

The winner of the Open Championship receives The Golf Champion Trophy, better known as the Claret Jug (because that's what it is, a particularly nice example of a silver jug used to serve claret).

A potted history of the Open Championship

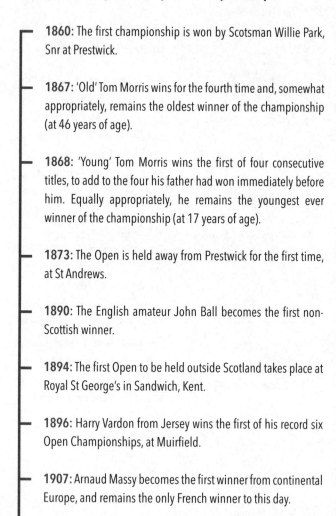

1860: The first championship is won by Scotsman Willie Park, Snr at Prestwick.

1867: 'Old' Tom Morris wins for the fourth time and, somewhat appropriately, remains the oldest winner of the championship (at 46 years of age).

1868: 'Young' Tom Morris wins the first of four consecutive titles, to add to the four his father had won immediately before him. Equally appropriately, he remains the youngest ever winner of the championship (at 17 years of age).

1873: The Open is held away from Prestwick for the first time, at St Andrews.

1890: The English amateur John Ball becomes the first non-Scottish winner.

1894: The first Open to be held outside Scotland takes place at Royal St George's in Sandwich, Kent.

1896: Harry Vardon from Jersey wins the first of his record six Open Championships, at Muirfield.

1907: Arnaud Massy becomes the first winner from continental Europe, and remains the only French winner to this day.

1921: America gets its first sort-of-a-victory when St Andrews-born Jock Hutchison wins at his birthplace. He had become a naturalised US citizen the previous year.

1922: America gets its first proper win when US-born Walter Hagan wins at the Royal Liverpool Club.

1947: Fred Daly becomes the first Northern Irish winner.

1949: South African Bobby Locke becomes the first winner from the southern hemisphere.

1951: The championship is staged at Royal Portrush in Northern Ireland, the only time it has moved outside Scotland or England.

1963: New Zealander Bob Charles becomes the first left-hander to win any major championship when he wins the Open at Royal Lytham.

1992: Nick Faldo wins the third of his Open victories, at Muirfield, and remains the last Englishman to win the trophy.

1999: Paul Lawrie becomes the first Scot to win on home soil for almost 70 years with his victory at Carnoustie.

2000: Tiger Woods wins at St Andrews after shooting 19 under par, the lowest ever score against par at any major championship.

2003: American Ben Curtis wins on his debut after Danish player Thomas Bjorn throws away a two-stroke lead by taking three shots to get out of a bunker on the 16th at Royal St George's.

2007: Padraig Harrington becomes the first winner from the Republic of Ireland (and successfully defends his title the following year).

2009: Some 26 years after his fifth Open victory, Tom Watson, at the age of 59, has an eight-foot putt on the last hole at Turnberry to equal Harry Vardon's record of six Open Championships. He misses and loses the resultant play-off to fellow American Stewart Cink.

2011: Northern Irishman Darren Clarke becomes the first home winner for 12 years.

2012: South African Ernie Els wins his second Open ten years after his first.

2013: American Phil Mickelson finally wins his first Open Championship, having warmed up by winning his first Scottish Open the week before.

Most wins

6	Harry Vardon	Jersey	1896, 1898, 1899, 1903, 1911, 1914
5	John Henry Taylor	England	1894, 1895, 1900, 1909, 1913
5	James Braid	Scotland	1901, 1905, 1906, 1908, 1910
5	Peter Thomson	Australia	1954, 1955, 1956, 1958, 1965
5	Tom Watson	USA	1975, 1977, 1980, 1982, 1983
4	Willie Park, Snr	Scotland	1860, 1863, 1866, 1875
4	'Old' Tom Morris	Scotland	1861, 1862, 1864, 1867
4	'Young' Tom Morris	Scotland	1868, 1869, 1870, 1872

Note: Notable players to have won three times include Bobby Jones, Henry Cotton, Gary Player, Jack Nicklaus, Seve Ballesteros, Nick Faldo and Tiger Woods.

Open Championship trivia

The Open Championship is not referred to as the 'British Open', because there was originally no other Open Championship to distinguish it from. Americans refer to it as the 'British Open' in order to distinguish it from the 'US Open', but they're just being silly.

The first 12 Opens were all held at Prestwick, before a decision was taken to spread the cost and organisation of the championship with St Andrews and Musselburgh Links. In 1892, Muirfield became only the fourth course to be used for the championship in 32 years.

The current rotation of courses involves nine venues, five in Scotland (St Andrews, Carnoustie, Muirfield, Turnberry and Royal Troon) and four in England (Royal St George's, Royal Birkdale, Royal Lytham and St Annes, and Royal Liverpool). St Andrews hosts every five years and the other courses host about every ten years.

Jack Nicklaus finished as runner-up on no fewer than seven occasions, winning 'only three' Open Championships as a result.

When Phil Mickelson won the Open at Muirfield in 2013, the USA finally moved above Scotland in terms of overall wins (42–41). It is a gap that will probably grow in favour of the USA in the years ahead.

Greg Norman holds the record for lowest winning score (267), achieved at the 1993 Open at Royal St George's.

PGA Championship

Prize fund: *c.*$8 million
(£4.8 million)

Winner's purse: *c.*$1.5
million (£900,000)

Trophy: Wanamaker Trophy

Other spoils of victory:

Gold medal

Introduction

The last of the four majors to be played each year, the PGA Championship takes place at different venues (but mostly in the eastern half of the United States) in mid August. The most frequent venue (four times) has been Southern Hills Country Club in Tulsa, Oklahoma. The tournament was established in 1916 as a match-play event (round-by-round, man-to-man knockout), and changed to standard stroke play (fewest strokes taken over four rounds) in 1958. The trophy is named after the department store magnate, Rodman Wanamaker, who was the driving force behind the first championship. The PGA is the only major that does not invite amateur players to compete.

A potted history of the PGA Championship

1916: Englishman Jim Barnes wins the first PGA Championship in Bronxville, New York, and successfully defends his title three years later (after World War One had stopped play in the intervening two years).

1922: Gene Sarazen's win makes him the youngest ever winner of the trophy, at the age of just 20.

1927: Walter Hagen secures his record-breaking fifth (match-play) title.

1947: Australian Jim Ferrier becomes the only non-American to win between 1920 and 1961.

1958: American Dow Finsterwald wins the first stroke-play PGA after the format changes from match play.

1962: Gary Player wins the first of two titles, although his second wouldn't come for another ten years.

1968: Victory for Hungarian-American Julius Boros makes him the oldest ever winner of the trophy, at the age of 48.

1980: Jack Nicklaus equals Hagen's record of five championships.

1991: The surprise winner is big-hitting American John Daly, who had scraped into the tournament as ninth reserve.

2003: This year sees another surprise winner in American Shaun Micheel, at the time ranked 169th in the world. It remains his one and only PGA Tour victory.

2008: Irishman Padraig Harrington becomes the first European to win since 1919.

2009: South Korean Yang Yong-eun becomes the first Asian winner.

2012: Northern Irishman Rory McIlroy wins by a record eight-stroke margin to become the first UK winner since 1919.

Most wins

5	Walter Hagan	USA	1921, 1924, 1925, 1926, 1927
5	Jack Nicklaus	USA	1963, 1971, 1973, 1975, 1980
4	Tiger Woods	USA	1999, 2000, 2006, 2007
3	Gene Sarazen	USA	1922, 1923, 1933
3	Sam Snead	USA	1942, 1949, 1951

PGA Championship trivia

American domination of the PGA Championship has been such that they have won 78 times as at the end of 2013, compared to just 16 victories by non-Americans.

After winning in 1927, Walter Hagen became the only player in the twentieth century to win the same major championship in four consecutive years.

David Toms (USA) holds the record low score of 265 (a record that stands across all major championships), achieved when he won the title in 2001.

Tiger Woods won a play-off against fellow American Bob May in 2000, after both players had finished a record-breaking 18 strokes under par. Woods then repeated the 18-under feat when he won in 2006.

Tiger Woods is the only player to have successfully defended the title in stroke-play format the following year, and he has done it twice (in 2000 and in 2007).

Fore!

From zero to hero

In 1991, Zimbabwean Nick Price pulled out of the PGA Championship at the eleventh hour, because his wife was about to give birth. One by one, the nine reserves on standby were contacted and, one by one, they explained that they couldn't make it to the course at Crooked Stick, Indiana, in time for the tournament. The ninth and final reserve, John Daly, said he could, and he did. And he won the tournament, at 12 under par. Nick Price's caddie had stayed on to help him, not least because Daly didn't have time for a practice round on the notoriously difficult course.

His driving is unbelievable. I don't go that far on my holidays.
IAN BAKER-FINCH, AUSTRALIAN MAJOR WINNER, ON JOHN DALY

CHAPTER 9

THE RYDER CUP

I trust that the effect of this match will be to influence a cordial, friendly and peaceful feeling throughout the whole civilised world…

SAMUEL RYDER, ON HIS GRAND AMBITIONS FOR THE TOURNAMENT HE INSTIGATED

Introduction

The Ryder Cup is a biennial match-play team event between Europe and the USA, which in recent times has become one of the world's great sporting contests. It is named after English businessman Samuel Ryder, who donated the trophy for an unofficial event in 1926 between Britain and the USA at Wentworth Golf Club in Surrey (which Britain won). The event was such a success that Ryder suggested they do it again, and they have, roughly every two years since 1927. Across all Ryder Cups up to 2012, the USA are 25–12 ahead, but since the Great Britain & Ireland team was extended in 1979 to include players from continental Europe, Team Europe is 9–7 ahead.

The current format was settled in 1979, with all 12 members on each team playing in singles matches on the final day (Sunday) after two days of foursomes (where each team's pairing plays alternate shots with the same ball) and fourballs (where each team's pairing plays their own ball throughout).

The players receive no financial reward for playing in or even winning the Ryder Cup, but it is nonetheless a competition they all desperately want to be picked to play in. Who says that glory alone is not worth fighting for?

A potted history of the Ryder Cup

1926: The Roaring Twenties are in full swing as Walter Hagen claims he is bringing 'the most powerful team that ever left New York' over to Wentworth for a team match between British and American professionals. Hagen's team takes a 13–1 beating, but the Ryder Cup is born.

1927: The first official Ryder Cup is won easily by the Americans in Worcester, Massachusetts.

1929: Great Britain & Ireland win their first Ryder Cup on home soil, at Moortown Golf Club in Leeds.

1939: The matches scheduled to take place in Florida in November are cancelled immediately after Great Britain declares war on Germany on 3 September. The next Ryder Cup takes place in Oregon in 1947.

1969: One of the most competitive golfing contests ever, with 18 of the 32 matches at Royal Birkdale going to the last hole. The overall result is a draw after Jack Nicklaus generously concedes a two-foot putt to England's Tony Jacklin on the last green. In the event of a tie, the previous winners retain the trophy so the Ryder Cup goes back to America.

1989: A draw at the Belfry sees the only other tied Ryder Cup competition in its history. This time the Europeans get to hold on to the trophy because they had won it two years beforehand at Muirfield Village, Ohio.

1991: 'The War on the Shore': a narrow win for Team USA at Kiawah Island in South Carolina, remembered chiefly for heightened gamesmanship and tension on both sides, in part sparked by a running personal feud between Spaniard Seve Ballesteros and American Paul Azinger. Players on both sides were reduced to public displays of tears as the emotion of the occasion got to them.

1999: 'The Battle of Brookline': the USA team comes from behind to snatch victory for the first time in six years. In the final stages, hyperactive American players and fans display levels of exuberance not before seen on a golf course, causing some American players to apologise after the event for not adhering to the spirit of the game.

2001: The match gets postponed for a year in the immediate aftermath of the September 11 terrorist attacks in America and, as a consequence, it has been played in even-numbered years since 2002.

2002: The postponed 2001 matches are played at the original planned venue of the Belfry, with the same teams that had been selected in 2001. The display boards remain headed 'The 2001 Ryder Cup'.

2012: 'The Miracle at Medinah': an extraordinary comeback at the Medinah Country Club in Illinois, inspired most notably by England's Ian Poulter, sees Europe claw back from 10–4 down to win 14½–13½.

Ryder Cup trivia

Nick Faldo has made the most appearances (11) and scored the most points (25) on either side.

The only player with a 100 per cent record is American Jimmy Demaret with six points out of six between 1947 and 1951.

In 1993, American Ray Floyd became the oldest Ryder Cup player at the age of 51.

In 1999, Spaniard Sergio Garcia became the youngest ever Ryder Cup player at the age of 19.

Scot Colin Montgomerie remained unbeaten in eight Ryder Cup singles matches, with six wins and two halves.

Team Europe has won seven out of the last nine Ryder Cup matches.

Fore!

Presidents Cup

Since 1994, the USA and an International Team (comprising golfers from the Rest of the World minus Europe) have played in Ryder Cup format for the biennial Presidents Cup. The USA have won ten of the first 12 competitions, a sole win for the Internationals coming in 1998 at Royal Melbourne, with one match drawn in South Africa in 2003.

Tiger Woods and Phil Mickelson have been the stars of the competition, and golfing legends to have captained the sides include Jack Nicklaus for the USA and Gary Player for the Internationals.

CHAPTER 10

THE WOMEN'S PROFESSIONAL GAME

Golf is a game of coordination, rhythm and grace.
Women have these to a high degree.

BABE ZAHARIAS, LEGENDARY GOLFER AND OLYMPIC ATHLETE

How it all began

We have already seen how Mary, Queen of Scots, started women's golf in controversial circumstances in sixteenth-century Scotland, but it was 1867 before the first golf club for women opened in (no prizes for guessing) St Andrews. The Ladies' Golf Union (LGU) followed in 1893 and still remains the governing body for women golfers in Great Britain and Ireland. The LGU also administers the Women's British Open each year.

On the other side of the pond in the same year that the LGU was formed, the first women's course in America was opened at Shinnecock Hills. In 1944, American women finally got their own governing body with the arrival of the Women's Professional Golf Association (WPGA), which was renamed the Ladies' Professional Golf Association (LPGA) in 1950. Today the LPGA continues to run the LPGA Tour in America, including the three LPGA major championships held in that country.

American domination

American players enjoyed utter domination of women's golf for most of the twentieth century. Patty Berg won 15 majors between 1937 and 1958, Mickey Wright won 13 between 1958 and 1966, and Louise Suggs won 11 between 1946 and 1959. With one notable exception, Americans also topped the LPGA money-winning list from its inception in 1950 until 1993, including a staggering eight out of nine years between 1965 and 1973 for Kathy Whitworth. The notable exception was Ayako Okamoto, a Japanese left-handed softball superstar who transformed herself into a right-handed golfing superstar good enough to top the LPGA money-winning list in 1987.

The changing of the guard

In 1994, everything changed. Forever. England's Laura Davies topped the money-winning list and no American golfer has done so since. It turned out that Davies was paving the way for Sweden's Annika Sörenstam, who topped the list eight times between 1995 and 2005, Australia's Karrie Webb (1996, 1999, 2000), and Mexican Lorena Ochoa (2006, 2007, 2008). And then, just when the Americans were thinking it probably couldn't get much worse, the Asian sorority arrived. South Korean women topped the list for four out of the next five years, interrupted only by Taiwanese player Yani Tseng in 2011. Major trophies also started to cross the Atlantic and then Pacific Oceans with alarming regularity – Sörenstam ended up with ten majors to her name, Webb seven and Tseng five. Se-Ri Pak, the first South Korean to arrive on the scene (in 1998), has also won five.

South Korean domination

And South Korea looks set to take over the women's game for the foreseeable future, with four players in the world's top ten, and eight in the top 20, at the start of 2014. Their contingent includes Inbee Park, who became world number one in 2013, a year in which she won three majors. South Korean golfers have already won more major championships (17) than any other country outside the USA, having overtaken Sweden's total of 14 in the last year. But they have some way to go to catch the USA as far as the record books are concerned, because American women have amassed 195 major titles, even if they did win most of those before the rest of the world arrived to spoil their party.

Major championships

As of 2014, there are five extant majors:

Kraft Nabisco Championship (since 1972)

Founded in 1972 as the magnificently named Colgate-Dinah Shore Winner's Circle after the American entertainer who founded it (and, I assume, the toothpaste she swore by), it became an LPGA major in 1983 when it was reincarnated as the Nabisco Dinah Shore (after the American entertainer and, I assume, her favourite cookies). Always held at the Mission Hills Country Club in California in the spring, it is the first women's major of the year.

> ### Fore!
>
> #### Ladies of the lake
>
> *Just as the iconic image of the men's first major of the year is the green jacket awarded to the Masters winner, the women's equivalent is the image of the Kraft Nabisco winner jumping into the pond beside the 18th green (although in 1998, Pat Hurst went in only up to her knees as she couldn't swim).*

US Women's Open Championship (since 1946)

The oldest of the women's majors, the championship was dominated in its first four decades by home-grown players. After the USA (with 49 wins at the time of writing), South Korea comes second with seven victories, including five out of six between 2008 and 2013.

Open means open!

The US Women's Open is open to all amateur and professional golfers, irrespective of age. The youngest-ever qualifier was 12-year-old American Lexi Thomas in 2007, and the youngest winner to date is South Korean Inbee Park in 2008, aged just 19.

LPGA Championship (since 1955)

The second oldest of the women's majors, this championship was also dominated by Americans up to the end of the twentieth century. In a remarkable turnaround since then, no American won the title between 2000 and 2010. South Korean and Swedish players have both now won on four occasions, but they are still a long way behind the Americans, who had won 40 times before the overseas contingent arrived in force.

Women's British Open (since 1976)

Started as a Ladies' European Tour major in 1976 and became a recognised LPGA major in 2001. Americans top the overall list of winners, but honours are more evenly spread across the golfers of the world than is the case with the American majors. American women have won on ten occasions, followed by England (seven wins by seven different players), Australia (five), South Korea and Sweden (four apiece).

Fore!

Mum's the word!

Scot Catriona Matthew became the first player from the 'home of golf' to win a women's major championship when she won the Women's British Open at Royal Lytham & St Annes in 2009. The Edinburgh-born golfer became champion just 11 weeks after giving birth to her second daughter, and only three weeks short of her 40th birthday.

Evian Championship (since 1994)

Established as a Ladies' European Tour event in 1994, it became the LPGA's fifth major in 2013. It is played each year at the Evian Resort Golf Club in France, 480 metres (1,575 feet) above nearby Lake Geneva, making it the first golfing major ever to be staged in continental Europe. Swedish players have won the most titles (six), followed by Japan (three) and Australia (three).

Fore!

The age of legends

In 2001, the Women's Senior Golf Tour was founded by the LPGA, for golfers aged 45 and over. In 2006, it was rebranded the Legends Tour, presumably to allow the participants to feel less senior and more legendary – in other words, for the same reason the Men's Seniors Tour was rebranded the Champions Tour.

Solheim Cup

The other major event in the women's professional golfing calendar, at least if you're European or American, is the biennial Solheim Cup, the women's match-play equivalent of the Ryder Cup. It was founded in 1990 by Karsten Solheim, a Norwegian-American golf club designer, who invented the centre-shafted putter and whose company, Karsten Manufacturing, is rather better known by its brand name of PING.

Of the 13 matches held up to 2013, USA have won eight and Europe five. England's Laura Davies has appeared the most times (12) and has won the most points of any individual golfer. The undoubted highlight for the European team was the stunning victory they secured in 2013 at the Colorado Golf Club, providing as it did a number of 'firsts':

- The first time they had retained the cup (having won in 2011 in Ireland).

- The biggest winning margin in the history of the competition (18–10).

- Their first victory on American soil.

- The first player to score the maximum five points in a single competition (Sweden's Caroline Hedwall).

- The first hole-in-one in the competition (Sweden's Anna Nordqvist).

- The youngest ever team member on either side (England's Charley Hull, aged 17, who won her singles match 5 & 4 against top American Paula Creamer).

A quick who's who of women's golf

Patty Berg

One of the pioneers of women's professional golf, Berg won 15 major titles, including the first ever women's major, the 1946 US Women's Open. She had turned professional in 1940 but put her fledgling career on hold while she served with the US Marines in World War Two.

Babe Zaharias

Not just one of the best golfers of all time, with ten major championships between 1940 and 1954, but also one of the best athletes of all time. By the time she took up golf, she had already won three medals at the 1932 Olympic Games in Los Angeles (gold in the javelin and 80-metres hurdles, silver in the high jump), but even that isn't all. In 1939, *Time* magazine described her as 'a famed woman athlete, 1932 Olympic Games track and field star, expert basketball player, golfer, javelin thrower, hurdler, high jumper, swimmer, baseball pitcher, football halfback, billiardist, tumbler, boxer, wrestler, fencer, weightlifter and adagio dancer'. Gulp!

Mickey Wright

Hailed by many as the greatest female golfer of the twentieth century, the American won 13 majors between 1958 and 1966, in spite of increasingly debilitating foot and wrist problems.. She is the only player in LPGA history to hold four majors simultaneously and she had achieved that by the age of 27.

Kathy Whitworth

The Texan won 88 LPGA events, more than any man or woman on any Tour in the history of the game. She won a tournament in every year between 1962 and 1978, the longest winning streak in LPGA history, and notched up 11 holes-in-one during LPGA competitions, another record.

Jan Stephenson

Remembered as much for her deliberate glamour-girl image in the 1980s (she famously posed in a bathtub full of strategically placed golf balls) as for her skill on the golf course, the Aussie player won 16 LPGA Tour events including three majors. She also recorded eight holes-in-one in LPGA Tour competitions.

Laura Davies

Coventry-born Davies is the most successful English female golfer by some way, with 20 LPGA Tour victories and four major titles. She set an LPGA record in 2004 with 19 eagles in a single season. Also a serious football fan (see next page).

Fore!

She shoots, she scores!

Laura Davies was once fined by the Ladies' European Tour for not showing sufficient respect to a tournament she was playing in. An avid England and Liverpool football supporter, she was caught watching an England v Spain European Championship football match on a portable television during the final round of the 1996 Evian Masters in France. England beat Spain in a penalty shoot-out that afternoon, and Davies multitasked her way to victory by four strokes.

Annika Sörenstam

Arguably the greatest female golfer of all time, the Swedish superstar won ten major championships between 1995 and 2006. Others before her won more, but not in the ultra-competitive arena of the modern game. She is still the only player to have shot 59 in an LPGA Tour event.

Se-Ri Pak

She is the player who paved the way for the dozens of South Koreans who followed in her footsteps to the LPGA Tour. In 1998, at the age of 20, she became the youngest winner of the Women's US Open, and she added four more majors by 2006.

Michelle Wie

The Hawaiian-born child prodigy qualified for a USGA women's amateur event in 2000 at the age of ten, then went on to become the youngest player to win an amateur event, the youngest to qualify for and make the cut at an LPGA Tour event, and the youngest to play in the Curtis Cup. Then, a week before her 16th birthday, she turned professional.

She had broken so many records that she was hailed in a blaze of publicity as the best female golfer the world was ever likely to see, the Tiger Woods of women's golf. Eight years on, she has yet to realise that potential, having won just two LPGA Tour events and no majors.

Fore!

Playing with the boys

Michelle Wie played in eight men's PGA Tour events between 2004 and 2008. She came within a single stroke of making the cut in the 2004 Sony Open in Hawaii at the age of just 14, when she shot even-par 140 over two rounds, including a second-round 68, the lowest score achieved to date by a woman in a PGA Tour event.

Paula Creamer

Instantly recognisable as she always wears something pink, her adoring American fans have nicknamed her the 'Pink Panther'. She won her first LPGA Tour event when just 20 years old and won her first major (the Women's US Open) in 2010.

Yani Tseng

The Taiwanese golfer is the youngest player ever, male or female, to win five major championships, which she achieved by the tender age of 22. Those major victories included back-to-back Women's British Open wins in 2010 and 2011. She then spent the next two years ranked number one in the Women's World Golf Rankings.

Cheyenne Woods

Possibly one to watch if she pays enough attention to golfing tips from Uncle Tiger! Turned professional in 2012 and won her first significant trophy in 2014 (the Australian Ladies' Masters). It would, though, be quite ironic if a woman named Cheyenne turned out to be the cavalry coming over the hill to save American golf from overseas invaders.

CHAPTER 11

PRACTICE MAKES PERFECT

The more I practise, the luckier I get.

GARY PLAYER, SOUTH AFRICAN NINE-TIMES MAJOR WINNER

Introduction

Whatever standard of golf you play, you can be sure of one thing –
regular practice will improve your game. That is also why golf tuition
is big business, whether it comes in the form of books, manuals,
DVDs, online instruction, a visit to the range or a lesson from your
local pro. It is also why professional golfers spend at least as much
time practising as they do competing.

Top teachers

The top players demand the top teachers, some of whom have
become household names and very rich men in their own right:

David Leadbetter

The Englishman came to prominence in the 1980s when he stripped and rebuilt the swing of Nick Faldo, who then went on to win six majors. His list of pupils includes Nick Price, Greg Norman, Ernie Els and Michelle Wie. Unless you can afford over $1,000 (£600) for each hour of Leadbetter tuition, your name is not getting added to that list any time soon.

Butch Harmon

Considered by many to be the finest golf instructor in the known universe, the American is best known for having coached Tiger Woods from 1993 to 2004. Before then, he had cut his instructional teeth on Greg Norman in the early 1990s and King Hassan II of Morocco in the 1970s (as you do). His pupil list has extended to include Americans Phil Mickelson, Stewart Cink, Davis Love III, Fred Couples, Justin Leonard, Dustin Johnson and Natalie Gulbis, as well as Aussie Adam Scott and South African Ernie Els.

Jack Grout

The American who was Jack Nicklaus's first and only golf coach. I have nothing else to say.

Harvey Penick

Coach to many golfing stars, including Americans Ben Crenshaw, Tom Kite, Kathy Whitworth and Mickey Wright, and writer of the best-selling golf book of all time: *Harvey Penick's Little Red Book: Lessons and Teachings from a Lifetime in Golf*. Although a great all-round coach, he is remembered by many as the best ever teacher of the mental aspects of the game.

Fore!

This one's for you, coach

The day after serving as pallbearer at Harvey Penick's funeral in 1995, his long-time friend and student Ben Crenshaw set out determined to win his second Masters in Penick's honour. It was a tall order, at the age of 43 and 11 years on from his only other win. He won by a single stroke, becoming the second-oldest winner in the tournament's history, and probably the most determined.

Dos and don'ts

Back in the real world of unprofessional golf, we strive desperately to remember the dos and don'ts that will keep us out of serious trouble on the course. Writing as someone who has played most shots most ways (and even, very occasionally, correctly), I consider myself supremely well qualified to offer you some tips on what you should and should not do the next time you find yourself lining up a shot:

Do:

✓ Visualise the shot. You know you can do this! You did it already three years ago!

✓ Take dead aim (pretend there's a whole pound or dollar at stake if that helps you to concentrate).

✓ Take your best guess at the right club for the job in hand and then let it 'do the work' – it's why you paid a lot of money for it (and you're getting paid nothing).

✓ Keep your head down (but be aware that the only reason a pro tells you this is so that you can't see him laughing).

✓ Convert your body to a coiled spring with your backswing (or as coiled a spring as you can manage given your age and condition).

✓ Swing smoothly and follow through, holding the pose until you're absolutely sure the cameras have stopped clicking.

✓ Accept the applause for what it is. (In your head alone.)

Don't:

- ❌ Dwell on how badly you've played so far (worse things will almost certainly be happening at sea).

- ❌ Take advice from your playing partners (you know they only wish you harm).

- ❌ Try to show off by using less of a club than you know you really need, *especially* if your much younger opponent visibly sneers every time you reach into your bag.

- ❌ Try to hit the ball so hard that it will fly further than it ever has before (it won't).

- ❌ Blame the awful weather for the poor round you're having – just remember you're the moron who decided to play in driving wind and rain in the first place.

- ❌ Take three or four or five practice swings – just concentrate properly on the first one and move on with your life and everybody else's.

- ❌ Shout 'Oh, no!' (or your own vernacular equivalent) whenever your ball goes off in a direction you hadn't been hoping for.

- ❌ Take over four and a half hours to play a round of golf (unless you're a member of the Mayfield Golfing Society, in which case 'well done' for breaking that elusive five-hour barrier).

Just hit it!

There is an alternative school of thought that says don't bother with all that teaching nonsense. Just turn up and hit the ball. Believers of this school think that playing golf is all the practice you need; that playing the game itself is more real than the many forms of tuition that exist to make you spend a lot of money finding out why you're not a better golfer than you are; and that having too many 'swing thoughts' is more destructive than having none at all. As schools of thought go, you have to admit that it is not entirely without logic, especially if you play golf at the more confused end of the spectrum.

CHAPTER 12

HALL OF FAME

Sudden success in golf is like the sudden acquisition of wealth. It is apt to unsettle and deteriorate the character.

P. G. WODEHOUSE, ENGLISH HUMORIST, AUTHOR AND GOLF FANATIC

I could very easily come up with a hundred names to include in a golfing hall of fame, and I could argue all day about the criteria that should be applied to determine which golfers should make the top ten, but there's no time for all that, so here is my own biased list of ten of the greatest players to have walked the fairways:

Name: Jack Nicklaus

Born: 1940, in Upper Arlington, Ohio

Major championships: 18 (6 Masters, 4 US Opens, 3 Open Championships, 5 PGA Championships)

PGA Tour wins: 73

Nickname: The Golden Bear

There is no doubt in my mind that Jack Nicklaus remains the greatest golfer of all time. He wasn't just great; he was consistently great. In addition to winning more major championships than anyone else (18), he finished second 19 times and third nine times. And when he finished second or third, he didn't throw tantrums. He just carried on in the same composed, dignified manner that made him the best ambassador the game ever had.

The Golden Bear also had staying power. His first major win, the 1962 US Open, came when he was aged 22 and still the reigning US Amateur Champion. His 18th came with the 1986 Masters at the age of 46.

Name: 'Tiger' Woods
Born: 1975, in Cypress, California
Major championships: 14 (4 Masters, 3 US Opens, 3 Open Championships, 4 PGA Championships)
PGA Tour wins: 79
Nickname: Tiger

As a child prodigy, Eldrick Tont Woods needed a nickname fast. Putting against Bob Hope on television at the age of two, breaking 80 on a golf course by the age of eight, and breaking 70 by the time he was 12, he had broken pretty much all the junior and amateur records going by the time he turned professional at the age of 20.

Within a year (in 1997), he had won his first major, becoming the youngest ever winner of the Masters in the process. In 2001, he became the first man to hold all four major titles simultaneously, and the majors kept on coming, until he had bagged 14 of them by 2008. And then the wheels came off the wagon.

Rocked by the public scandal of extramarital affairs, his clean-cut image disappeared overnight and many of his sponsors headed for the hills. Although he has since regained the world number one spot, the majors continue to elude him and it looks less likely with each passing year that he will do what everyone once thought he would achieve with ease – surpass Jack Nicklaus's record of 18 major wins. Having said that, he is the only golfer in history to be ranked number one in the world whilst 'in a slump'.

Name: Tom Watson
   Born: 1949, in Kansas City, Missouri
      Major championships: 8 (2 Masters, 1 US Open, 5 Open Championships)
PGA Tour wins: 39
Nickname: Huckleberry Dillinger (but not for long)

Watson is the man who replaced Jack Nicklaus as world number one, and who pipped Nicklaus at the post for a number of his major victories. One of the greatest links golfers ever, Watson won the Open Championship at his first attempt in 1975 and five times in all. He literally came within inches of adding a sixth in 2009 at the age of 59. A true gentleman in the Nicklaus mould, he was one of the most popular golfers at home and abroad, and especially so with British fans.

Although some press tried to dub him 'Huckleberry Dillinger' in the early days, because his innocent face (Huckleberry) belied his killer instinct (Dillinger), it didn't stick because everyone just wanted to call him 'Tom'. I did once, in the closing stages of his head-to-head with Seve Ballesteros at St Andrews in 1984. 'Good luck, Tom' were my exact words as he strode up the 16th fairway. 'Thank you,' he replied with the half-smile of an innocent killer. Seve would beat him to the title within half an hour of our little chat, but I didn't mind because they were both my heroes.

Name: Severiano Ballesteros
Born: 1957, in Pedreña, Spain
Major championships: 5 (2 Masters, 3 Open Championships)
European Tour wins: 50
Nickname: Seve

The most famous and most popular European golfer of all time, but not just famous for what he achieved, famous also for having paved the way for others in Europe and beyond to follow his example of winning majors, of winning in America, and of beating Americans. He was the first European to win the Masters in 1980.

He had already set the golf world alight when he won his first Open in 1979 at Royal Lytham, after making birdie at the 16th hole of the final round in spite of having put his tee shot into a car park, which was typical of his cavalier playing style. He described the moment he sank a birdie putt on the last green to win his second Open at St Andrews in 1979 as the happiest moment of his life. Ever the showman, that was the moment when millions around the world watched him theatrically replace his trusty putter-sword in its scabbard as the ball dropped in the hole.

Seve helped the Europeans to five Ryder Cup victories, four times as a player and once as captain (at Valderrama). He won the World Match Play five times and notched up a record-breaking 50 European Tour wins.

Name: Nick Faldo
Born: 1957, Welwyn Garden City, Hertfordshire
Major championships: 6 (3 Masters, 3 Open
Championships)
European Tour wins: 30
Nickname: Nasty Nick/Nice Nick

A former carpet-fitter who achieved success at junior, amateur and professional levels before sacrificing two years in the mid eighties to rebuild his swing in a way that would allow him to compete at the highest levels of the game, i.e. he wanted a swing that he could win major championships with. It worked. In 1987, he won his first Open Championship after famously making par at every single hole of the last round while others around him faltered. That's what you call a swing that holds up under pressure.

He went on to win six majors and go down in history as the best British golfer of all time. He represented Europe in a record 11 Ryder Cups and amassed a record 25 points in the process. He won BBC Sports Personality of the Year in 1989, was awarded the MBE (Medal of the British Empire) in 1998, and was knighted by the Queen in 2009. Not bad for a carpet-fitter.

He was rather unkindly known during his playing years as 'Nasty Nick' because his single-minded focus on winning came across as intimidating to his fellow professionals, but he has since become 'Nice Nick' as a knowledgeable and genial TV golf commentator.

Name: Gary Player
Born: 1935, in Johannesburg, South Africa
Major championships: 9 (3 Masters, 1 US Open, 3 Open Championships, 2 PGA Championships)
PGA Tour wins: 24
Nickname: The Black Knight

Player is the only non-American ever to have won the career Grand Slam of all four major titles. As the winner of 165 tournaments across six continents over six decades, from his home base in Johannesburg, he is also considered to be the most travelled athlete in history, having logged over 15 million miles (25 million kilometres) in the pursuit of his chosen profession. His first major victory was the 1959 Open Championship at Muirfield and his last was the 1978 Masters. In 2000, he was voted South Africa's Sportsman of the Century. Along with Jack Nicklaus and Arnold Palmer, he was known as one of the 'Big Three' of his era.

He may have been one of the smallest of the top golfers, at only 1.68 metres (five foot six inches), but he was also one of the fittest, working out to the point of earning the nickname of 'Mr Fitness'. But he was more affectionately known as 'The Black Knight' on account of the black golfing attire he always wore, a habit supposedly formed in his attempts to reflect the fierce sun while playing on the Sunshine Tour, as his home Southern African tour has become known.

Name: Arnold Palmer
Born: 1929, in Latrobe, Pennsylvania
Major championships: 7 (4 Masters, 1 US Open, 2 Open Championships)
PGA Tour wins: 62
Nickname: The King

Known to his wide fan base (the self-styled 'Arnie's Army') as 'The King', Palmer was the first superstar of golf's television age when it began in the 1950s. He is considered to have popularised the game with the masses, in part due to his swashbuckling 'go-for-broke' playing style. It also helped that he was of humble background compared to most players of the time, and by the time he shot to superstardom, he had overcome polio and served three years in the United States Coast Guard.

He was credited with securing the status of the Open Championship, because he considered it one of the four ingredients of the elusive Grand Slam at a time when not many Americans were making the trip to Britain to compete in the tournament. Where Arnie went, the world followed, and he unsurprisingly became immensely popular with the British public. There was never a more appropriate winner of the Open Championship than Arnold Palmer in 1961 and 1962.

An avid pilot for over 50 years, he is further immortalised by the renaming in 1999 of his local airport in Latrobe as the Arnold Palmer Regional Airport.

Name: Phil Mickelson
Born: 1970, in San Diego, California
Major championships: 5 (3 Masters, 1 Open Championship, 1 PGA)
PGA Tour wins: 42
Nickname: Lefty

Phil Mickelson is naturally right-handed but he plays golf left-handed because he learned the game facing his father, i.e. by copying a mirror image of his father's right-handed swing.

After a successful collegiate and amateur career, Mickelson turned professional in 1992 and won a healthy number of PGA Tour events as he thrilled crowds with his soft touch around the greens in particular. But the majors just wouldn't come for 'Lefty' and it wasn't until victory in the 2004 Masters that he finally got the 'best player never to win a major' monkey off his back. He has made up for those 'lean years' since, adding two more Masters, one Open Championship and one PGA. In addition to his five major wins, he has finished runner-up six times in the US Open, the only major to have so far eluded him.

Name: Sam Snead
  Born: 1912, in Ashwood, Virginia
   Major championships: 7 (3 Masters, 1 Open Championship, 3 PGA Championships)
PGA Tour wins: 82
Nickname: Slammin' Sam

Remembered as much for his trademark straw hat as his record 82 PGA Tour wins and seven majors, many considered Sam Snead to have the perfect golf swing – elegant and seemingly effortless, it nonetheless generated enormous power and distance, especially into the wind, hence the 'Slammin' Sam' nickname. He was just as effective with his short game and loved to experiment with different styles – he pioneered the use of a sand iron to get out of thick rough and he adopted a croquet-style putting stroke in the 1960s until the USGA banned it, whereupon he had a go at 'side-saddle' for a while (crouching down facing the ball with his feet angled towards the hole).

His professional career lasted 53 years. He won his first Tour event in 1936, became the oldest player (at 52) to win a Tour event in 1965, and became the youngest golfer to shoot his age (67) in a Tour event in 1979. In 1950, he averaged 69.23 per round for the year, an average-score record that held for 50 years until Tiger Woods finally usurped it in 2000.

Name: Ben Hogan

Born: 1912, in Stephenville, Texas

Major championships: 9 (2 Masters, 4 US Opens, 1 Open Championship, 2 PGA Championships)

PGA Tour wins: 64

Nickname: The Wee Iceman (in Scotland) or The Hawk (in the USA)

Ben Hogan completes my top ten, not just for what he achieved on the golf course, but also for the sheer guts of the man in overcoming more obstacles than anyone should have to overcome in a single lifetime.

Having watched his father shoot himself dead when he was aged nine, he took a job as a golf caddy to help the family make ends meet. He learned to play golf, but not that well. He turned professional in 1930 anyway and won nothing for ten years, primarily because he had a dreadful hook that prevented him hitting the ball straight. He went broke more than once.

Having cured his hook, he finally started winning tournaments in 1940, only for his career to be upended by World War Two, during which he served in the US Air Force. After the war he suddenly started winning major championships and had three in the bag when he and his wife only just survived a head-on collision with a Greyhound bus. With various bones broken, doctors told him that he might not walk again. They were wrong. Returning to the game in 1950, he limped his way to another six major championships.

Note: I apologise if I have missed out your particular all-time favourite golfer. If it helps at all, I feel particularly guilty about having left out Harry Vardon, Gene Sarazen, Walter Hagan, Byron Nelson, Lee Trevino and Rory McIlroy (even if he is a bit young for a hall of fame). I would definitely have included Bobby Jones if I had not already written about him in the chapter headed 'The amateur game'.

CHAPTER 13

CELEBRITY SWINGERS

I know I'm getting better at golf because I'm hitting fewer spectators.
  Gerald Ford, US president and wayward golfer

This chapter looks at the myriad famous people who have fallen in love with the game of golf, from rock and pop stars to actors and writers, from royals and world leaders to sportsmen and women; from entrepreneurs to a supermodel action girl.

 Musicians and singers

Alice Cooper

Alice Cooper, Golf Monster is the autobiography that the 'shock rock' star wrote to explain how he managed to kick his alcohol habit by getting up at 7 a.m. every morning to play 36 holes of golf. In between rounds, he drinks Diet Coke to wash down his clubhouse lunch, which consists of live chicken in a basket with a side order of still-warm snakes (I might have made that bit up).

Justin Timberlake

A low-handicapper who plays between concerts when he is on tour and who has eagled the par-five 13th hole at Augusta National despite hitting his drive behind a tree. When local property dealers threatened to buy up his home course, Mirimichi, in Memphis, Tennessee, he bought it himself to safeguard its future as a club.

Meat Loaf

Mr Loaf took time off from recording *Bat Out of Hell III* in 2006 to play in a celebrity 'Ryder Cup' at Celtic Manor in Wales, but found himself on the losing side after Bruce Forsyth sank the winning putt for Team Europe.

Other famous golfing musicians/singers include:

- Harry Styles (plays in between concerts with fellow band member Niall Horan – the One Direction the boys hope for is straight down the middle).

- Celine Dion (so passionate about the game that the Canadian songstress has opened her own course, Le Mirage, in Terrebonne, near Montreal).

- Snoop Dogg (the hip hop icon shoots about 90 when he's not doing his gangsta thing in the hood).

- Willie Nelson (when not writing or performing songs or campaigning to get marijuana legalised, the Country Music Hall of Fame member likes to unwind on the golf course).

○ Shakira (the Colombian singer knows when she hasn't swung properly through the ball because her hips don't lie).

○ Bob Dylan (no one really understood how the influential singer/songwriter managed to capture the anguish of a tortured human soul until it was discovered he played golf).

 Actors

Kiefer Sutherland

In between bouts of single-handedly defeating terrorism and saving the president of the free world, always within 24 hours, Jack Bauer likes to relax away from all that violence with a leisurely round of golf.

Samuel L. Jackson

The Mr Cool of the film world, Samuel Leroy Jackson won't agree to make a movie unless his contract allows him to play golf twice a week. Because he had to learn 109 different movements when preparing for *Star Wars II*, he carried his lightsaber in his golf bag for a while so that he could practise some shapes on the tee while waiting for the group ahead to clear the hole.

Other famous golfing actors include:

- Hugh Grant (one of the best golfers on the celebrity circuit, the film star learned the dark art with golfing gurus Steve Gould and Dave Wilkinson at their Knightsbridge Golf School).
- Teri Hatcher (still dusts down the clubs for the odd celebrity tournament when she's not desperately trying to be a housewife on Wisteria Lane).
- Catherine Zeta Jones (the Welsh Hollywood actress is an avid golfer often seen on the course with her husband, Mr Zeta Jones – there is a much smaller gap between their handicaps than their ages).
- Andy Garcia (the Cuban American A-list film star doesn't just show up for pro-ams – he wins them).
- James Nesbitt (the Belfast-born actor started playing at Royal Portrush in his twenties).
- Marilyn Monroe (took golf lessons during breaks from filming, and famously said that she went to bed wearing nothing but a number 5-iron).

Writers

Ian Fleming

English author, journalist and naval intelligence officer Ian Lancaster Fleming was a member for years at Royal St George's, the iconic links course at Sandwich in Kent that has hosted the Open Championship on 14 occasions. His wife often complained that he spent too much time playing golf and afterwards knocking back pink gins in the clubhouse. (Who did he think he was, James Bond?) He was nominated as club captain the day before he died at the age of just 56 in 1964.

Sir Arthur Conan Doyle

The creator of Sherlock Holmes was a keen sportsman who excelled at football as a goalkeeper and at cricket as a first-class batsman, but golf was to become his abiding sporting love. He was a member at Crowborough Beacon in East Sussex for a number of years, and club captain there in 1910 (with Mrs Conan Doyle following up as Ladies' Captain in 1911). A firm believer in the afterlife, he made a pact with his son, Kingsley, as the latter was leaving to fight in World War One, that if Kingsley did not survive the war, they would meet again on what is now the club's fourth green on the anniversary of Kingsley's death. His son did not survive and it is said that at least Sir Arthur kept the appointment.

P. G. Wodehouse

Sir Pelham Grenville Wodehouse played golf into his 90s and wrote a total of 31 short golf stories, collected together in *The Golf Omnibus*, which Wodehouse dedicated to the immortal memory of three Scottish golfers who were imprisoned in Edinburgh at the turn of the seventeenth century for the crime of 'playing of the gowff on the links of Leith every Sabbath the time of the sermonses'.

Other famous golfing writers include:

- Harper Lee (American author of *To Kill a Mockingbird* who claims to have done her most creative thinking on the golf course).
- A. A. Milne (English author, creator of Winnie the Pooh, and 18-handicap golfer).
- James Patterson (the American author is a golf addict who plays three or four mornings a week before settling down to the business of writing best-selling thrillers).

Entrepreneurs

Bill Gates

It has often been said that money can't buy exclusive membership at Augusta National in Georgia, but they have a lot of very wealthy members. Mr Microsoft himself became one of Augusta's 300 members in 2002 and plays there regularly with his fellow top-of-the-rich-list buddy, Warren Buffet. I wonder what stakes they play for? 'Fifty cents on the front nine, fifty cents on the back nine, and fifty cents for the game. That sound OK to you, Warren?'

Donald Trump

The business magnate is a low-handicap golfer who loves the game so much that he has built his own staggeringly beautiful five-star golf estate in Aberdeenshire. Never one for humility (he considers himself a worthy candidate to become president of the United States one day), he has named his golf venture the Trump International Golf Links. Perhaps one day he imagines that people will speak the name with the same hushed tones of reverence currently reserved for the Royal and Ancient Golf Club of St Andrews. He may be disappointed.

Sportsmen and women

Eve Muirhead

The Scottish ice maiden skippered Team GB to win the Curling World Championships in 2013 and to a bronze medal at the 2014 Sochi Winter Olympics. She had previously turned down the chance to become a professional golfer, having been offered scholarships at two American universities, and she still plays off scratch at Pitlochry Golf Course. As if all that isn't talent enough, she is also an accomplished bagpiper, having piped at four world championships.

Rafael Nadal

When not playing tennis, the multiple-Grand-Slam-winning 'King of Clay' keeps his swing smooth on the course. In 2013, he teamed up with his friend, Masters-winning Ryder Cup captain José María Olazábal, to host and take part in the Olazábal Nadal Invitational tournament to raise money for their charitable foundations.

Other famous golfing sportsmen and women include:

- Sir Steve Redgrave (now finding out the hard way that it is much harder to get your golf handicap into single figures than it is to win five consecutive Olympic rowing gold medals).
- Ana Ivanovic (the Serbian former world number one tennis player took up golf when she started dating Adam Scott, the first Australian golfer to win the Masters).
- A. P. McCoy (the perennial champion jockey has played with Tiger Woods at a pro-am tournament at Adare Manor in County Limerick, Ireland).
- Ben Ainslie (the most successful Olympic sailor of all time and now an America's Cup hero to boot, Ainslie is one of the few golfers who don't mind when the wind gets up a bit).
- Steven Gerrard (the Liverpool and England legend is one of many top-level footballers who relax on the golf course in between matches).

👑 Royals and world leaders

Prince Andrew

His Royal Highness The Prince Andrew Albert Christian Edward has many titles, including Duke of York, Earl of Inverness, Baron Killyleagh, Knight Companion of the Most Noble Order of the Garter, Knight Grand Cross of the Royal Victorian Order, and Aide-de-Camp to Her Majesty. But the one he is most proud of, as a low-handicap golfer, is Captain of the Royal and Ancient Golf Club of St Andrews 2003–2004.

Edward VIII

A keen and extremely competent golfer as the Prince of Wales, Edward didn't get much time to play during his troubled year as King Edward VIII in 1936. In an attempt to get his handicap back down (and not, as many of the British establishment believed, to marry 'that dreadful American woman'), he abdicated and accepted the post of Governor of the Bahamas. As governing the Bahamas took about an hour a day, the now Duke of Windsor was soon back in full swing.

Kim Jong-il

According to his official biographer, the former leader of North Korea decided to play his first round of golf in 1994 and shot a 38-under-par round of just 34 that included 11 holes-in-one. Satisfied that he had mastered the game, he never lifted a club again, and the world will never know how just good a golfer he might have become if he had carried on playing.

Other famous golfing world leaders include:

- Winston Churchill (apparently he never did get much good at the game of golf, but he did enjoy the 19th-hole brandies and cigars).
- David Lloyd George (the first Welsh prime minister of the United Kingdom even had a house built overlooking his beloved Walton Heath Golf Club in Surrey).
- Barack Obama (being president of the USA has not prevented him from playing a couple of hundred rounds of golf since he took office).

Supermodel action girl

Jodie Kidd

After a childhood of competitive showjumping, lacrosse, athletics, swimming and high jump, followed by a period of wild supermodel partying, action girl Jodie Kidd has now settled down to the marginally less hectic lifestyle of polo playing, rally driving, acting, modelling, designing and (got there in the end) golf! A combination of the skill to wear golf attire well (a skill which most golfers lack) and an 18 handicap make Kidd a firm favourite on the celebrity fundraising golf circuit.

CHAPTER 14

GOLF ON FILM

The trailer

Golf is attractive to film-makers, because it contains all the story ingredients they need. Victory against the odds, personal disaster, humour, local boy done good – just take your pick, Mr Movie Director. From rom-coms to biopics, from 007 to Carl Spackler, here are my top ten classic portrayals of golf on film for your viewing pleasure:

Caddyshack (1980) Director: Harold Ramis

Chevy Chase was the star that romped through the hilarious goings-on at the exclusive Bushwood Country Club, but this cult movie may just be best remembered for Bill Murray's portrayal of the unstable Carl Spackler, the assistant greenkeeper licensed to kill gophers by the government of the United Nations. Before he gets round to blowing up everything on the golf course (except, of course, the gopher), Murray delivers his imaginary 'Cinderella story' golf moment as he lops the heads off the country club's perfectly manicured flowers one by one.

Happy Gilmore (1996) Director: Dennis Dugan

Considered one of Adam Sandler's most memorable performances, the ex-hockey player Happy Gilmore is credited with inventing the 'running-start golf swing' as he tries against great odds to win enough money at golf to stop the IRS evicting his elderly grandmother from her home. Aided by his one-handed golf coach 'Chubbs' (Carl Weathers), what could possibly go wrong? Chubbs is an ex-pro whose career ended when an alligator bit his hand off, so Happy later kills the alligator in revenge and presents Chubbs with its head, whereupon a shocked Chubbs reels backward and falls out of an open window to his death. You had to be there.

Tin Cup (1996) Director: Ron Shelton

Easily Kevin Costner's greatest role, given the total absence of a game of golf in *The Bodyguard*, *Dances with Wolves* and *Robin Hood: Prince of Thieves*. Roy 'Tin Cup' McAvoy, a former golfing prodigy and now unambitious golf instructor at his own driving range, is goaded by a rival (Don Johnson) into entering the US Open. Rene Russo plays the girl who messes with the boys' heads and there are cameo roles in this rom-com drama for some real-life golfing greats, including Phil Mickelson, Craig Stadler, Johnny Miller, Lee Janzen and Fred Couples.

The Legend of Bagger Vance (2000) Director: Robert Redford

Set in 1930s Savannah, this film sees Rannulph Junuh (Matt Damon) overcome his World War One demons and rediscover his golfing mojo with the help of mysterious caddy-guru Bagger Vance (Will Smith). Pitted against legendary golfers Bobby Jones and Walter Hagan, Junuh ultimately wins back his pride when he comes from a long way back to draw level with the two of them by the end of the three-day match. In the process, he also rather neatly wins back the love of his life, Adele Invergordon (Charlize Theron).

Goldfinger (1964) Director: Guy Hamilton

Who could forget the game of high stakes played at the fictional Royal St Marks (which was in fact Stoke Park in Buckinghamshire) between Auric Goldfinger and a nine-handicap James Bond? Goldfinger's bowler-hatted henchman Oddjob, caddying for his master, crushes a golf ball in one hand in an attempt to put the wind up 007, which might have worked on, say, Roger Moore, but it was never going to work on Sean Connery (as Oddjob was to find out to his cost when he was later sucked out of the aircraft window that 007 had stabbed open with his special aircraft-window-stabbing knife). The match was, of course, won by 007 in spite of Goldfinger and Oddjob's many attempts to cheat their way to victory.

The 51st State (aka Formula 51) (2001) Director: *Ronny Yu*

Real-life golfing fanatic Samuel L. Jackson was never more in his element. His character is the drug-dealing, kilt-wearing, baddie-bashing character Elmo McElroy, an American who finds himself misplaced in the Liverpool underworld, and who just happens to carry his golf bag everywhere he goes. It turns out that his golf clubs double up as pretty effective weapons for bashing Scousers, but he also manages to get in some proper golf practice while escaping from some of the baddies on a scrap-metal barge (as you do).

The Greatest Game Ever Played (2005) Director: *Bill Paxton*

A true story set in 1913 when 20-year-old Francis Ouimet (played by Shia LaBoeuf) defied great odds to become the first amateur to win the US Open. Ouimet had been born on the wrong side of the tracks in Brookline, Massachusetts, where the US Open was held that year, and astonished the golfing world by beating world-famous golfers Ted Ray and Harry Vardon in an 18-hole play-off. His caddy for the tournament was ten-year-old Eddie Lowery, who had skipped school in the hope of earning a few dollars. As Ouimet himself received no prize money for winning the Open as an amateur, a whip-round was arranged amongst the spectators to ensure that the caddy at least got something for his efforts.

Bobby Jones: Stroke of Genius (2004) *Director: Rowdy Herrington*

This biopic tells the story of the greatest amateur to have graced the planet with his golfing genius. It relates how Jones had to overcome an unforgiving perfectionist tendency and a fierce temper to become the best golfer in the world, only to find when he got there that his success was destroying the lives of those around him. Jim Caviezel may have had the leading role as Bobby Jones, but he had an unexpected co-star in the Old Course at St Andrews. It was the first time that the R & A had ever allowed their hallowed turf to be used as a movie location. And it shone.

Seven Days in Utopia (2011) *Director: Matt Russell*

An embarrassing tournament leads to a public meltdown for wet-behind-the-ears pro golfer Luke Chisholm (Lucas Black), during which he crashes on to the property of eccentric Texan rancher Johnny Crawford (Robert Duvall). As fate would have it, Crawford is a former pro golfer who sees much of himself in the young Luke and decides to take him under his wing and sort out his head and his golf swing. This might be a 'good for the soul' kind of movie, but it doesn't go all cheesy in the way that these movies often do. You might even pick up some tips on how to improve your mental game. There are cameo roles for American pros Rich Beem, Stewart Cink and Rickie Fowler as themselves, and, in an inspirational moment of casting, a silent part for South Korean golfer K. J. Choi as golfer T. K. Oh.

Miracle on the 17th Green (2005) *Director: Michael Switzer*

This made-for-TV film adaptation of James Patterson's book of the same name follows the story of middle-aged advertising executive Travis McKinley (played by Robert Urich), who goes to play golf on Christmas Day to escape the irritations of his family and suddenly finds himself 'in the zone' for the first time in his life. He misses Christmas dinner and suffers the inevitable domestic consequences. Seemingly unable to do anything right in his personal life, but suddenly able to do nothing wrong on the golf course, he turns pro and soon finds himself playing the final round of the PGA Senior Open at Pebble Beach with his heroes Jack Nicklaus and Ray Floyd. And then something happens on the 17th hole that will change Travis, and his family, forever...

CHAPTER 15

WEIRD AND WONDERFUL GOLF FACTS

Man blames fate for all other accidents, but feels
personally responsible for a hole-in-one.

MARTHA BECKMAN, AMERICAN WRITER

The gifts are on me!

If you think it's bad having to buy a round of drinks for everyone in the clubhouse every time you get a hole-in-one, spare a thought for your fellow Japanese golfers. Many of them take out 'hole-in-one insurance', because if they hit a hole-in-one it is customary to share their good luck by throwing a party complete with gifts for all their friends.

Shaken *and* stirred

English golfer John Hudson bagged himself a hole-in-one at the par-three 12th hole playing the 1971 Martini International at Royal Norwich Golf Club in England. Just to prove it wasn't a fluke, he holed out with his driver at the next (par-four) hole. Just in case you're wondering, the odds against this happening are quite high.

Well, we've all done that!

While playing the 1992 Texas Open at Oak Hills Country Club in San Antonio, American Carl Cooper hit his drive over 750 yards at the third hole. The par-four hole was only 456 yards long but Cooper had made the classic mistake of not allowing for his ball hitting a downhill concrete buggy path followed by a never-ending on-course maintenance road. He took 4-iron, 8-iron and wedge to come back 300 yards to the third green, where he two-putted for a double bogey.

Catch a grip, Tommy!

At the 1978 Masters, Japanese golfer Tommy Nakajima took an unprecedented 13 strokes on the par-five 13th hole. After hitting into Rae's Creek, he unwisely chose to play the ball from the water rather than take the ball back to the dropping zone and incur a one-stroke penalty. The ball splashed up when he hit it and it landed on his foot, incurring a two-stroke penalty and leaving him in no better a position. He then dropped his club into the creek, incurring another two-stroke penalty, leading in the end to the highest single-hole score in the history of the Masters.

The Sands of Nakajima

Later that same year, Nakajima was in contention at the Open Championship on the third day at St Andrews until he putted off the green into the notoriously deep Road Hole bunker at the 17th. He took four attempts to get back up out of the sand so that he could finally resume putting. The British tabloids' headline pretty much wrote itself the next morning.

One-club wonder

The lowest golf score over 18 holes using only one club was a two-under-par 70 by American Thad Daber, using his 6-iron at the 1987 World One Club Championship at Lochmere Golf Club in North Carolina.

Golf at the Olympics

Golf first appeared as an Olympic event at the Paris Games in 1900, and last appeared as an Olympic event at the St Louis Games of 1904 in Missouri. It will finally reappear at Rio de Janeiro in 2016 and is also scheduled to be an event at the 2020 Games in Tokyo.

Fly Delta

The ravine that runs alongside the second hole at Augusta National is known by Masters competitors as the 'Delta ticket counter', because a visit there in the first couple of days of the tournament can lead to a rescheduling of a player's flight home.

Alpha, Bravo, Charlie...

Golf is so important that it is the only sport to feature in the NATO phonetic alphabet used around the world for radio communication (particularly in the aviation industry).

How to really melt a drive

Russian cosmonaut Mikhail Tyurin, ably assisted by his American caddy, Commander Michael Lopez-Alegria, teed off during a spacewalk outside the International Space Station in 2006. NASA estimated that the ball orbited for three days before burning up in the atmosphere – a distance of 1.26 million miles (2.02 million kilometres).

Clubbing it round London

The fastest marathon while dressed as a golfer was achieved in 3 hours 43 minutes 20 seconds by Belgian Bertrand Bodson at the 2010 London Marathon. Bodson carried a golf club with him throughout the race.

The younger, the better

The youngest golfer to record a hole-in-one is American Christian Carpenter, who was aged 4 years 195 days when he achieved the feat at the Mountain View Golf Club, North Carolina, in 1999. He had to buy everyone in the clubhouse a milkshake.

Designer balls

Golf balls have anywhere between 300 and 500 dimples depending on which company designs the ball. Apparently the ideal ball has between 380 and 432 dimples so be sure to count carefully before you next tee up.

Lost cause

It is estimated that around 500 million golf balls are lost each year. I should know. I've lost most of them.

A pound's a pound

In a sonar search for the Loch Ness Monster in 2009, scientists instead found over a hundred thousand golf balls at the bottom of the 21-square-mile loch, suggesting that Scots have been using it as a free driving range. Or that the Loch Ness Monster is a keen golfer.

Watch the birdie!

At the 1998 Players Championship a gull decided to snatch American Steve Lowery's ball from the famous island green at the par-three 17th hole at Sawgrass. After several attempts, it finally picked it up in its beak and flew off, but it couldn't take the weight and dropped it into the water that surrounds the green. A lot of golf balls end up in that watery grave each year but not many spend a few minutes on the green before dropping in. Lowery was allowed to place another ball where the original one had landed but ironically missed his birdie putt.

Making space for golf

In 1971, Apollo 14 astronaut Alan Shepard became the fifth man to walk on the moon and, much more significantly, became the first man to play golf there. His makeshift club was a Wilson 6-iron head attached to the handle of a lunar-sample scoop. On account of his huge gloves and rigid spacesuit, he had to swing the 'club' with one hand, but he nonetheless struck the second shot, as he himself later described it, 'miles and miles and miles'.

Is it witchcraft?

Until 2003 only one left-handed golfer had ever won a major championship. That golfer was New Zealander Bob Charles, who won the Open Championship in 1963, i.e. not long after they had stopped burning left-handed people at the stake for witchcraft. Since Canadian leftie Mike Weir opened the floodgates by winning the Masters in 2003, however, Phil Mickelson (with five majors) and Bubba Watson have kept the sinister victories coming. Seven left-handed major wins in the 11 years from 2003 to 2013 is clearly unnatural, but it is not for me to suggest that witchcraft may once more be at play.

Alliss-isms

Ex-professional golfer and popular television commentator Peter Alliss is known for sometimes letting his tongue run ahead of his brain. Here are just some of the Englishman's finest commentating moments:

'They'll be chasing kangaroos round the coolabong tonight.'
(When Australian Adam Scott won the 2013 Masters.)

'Not in those trousers, sir. Not at this club. Try the municipal course.'

'A little premature, my cock-a-leekie.'
(When Tiger Woods missed a putt on the low side.)

'He's at that dangerous age – mid to late forties – when things start to happen to the human body.'

'As the cock crows, it's only about two hundred yards.'

'It's a funny old game. One day you're a statue. The next you're a pigeon.'

'If you can imagine a clock face – the wind is coming from about half past two.'

'He hasn't got any good points to his swing that a bit of tuition couldn't ruin.'

'I haven't seen a grip like that since they closed the gents at King's Cross station.'

'One good thing about the rain in Scotland – most of it ends up as Scotch.'

'In technical terms, he's making a real pig's ear of this hole.'

'It's like turning up to hear Pavarotti sing and finding
out he has laryngitis.'
(Describing Tiger Woods's 81 in the third round of the
2002 Open Championship.)

'Have at thee, Sir Percy!'
(After Sergio Garcia drove the green at the par-four
tenth at the Belfry.)

Peter Alliss: 'What do you think of the climax of this tournament?'
Peter Thomson: 'I'm speechless.'
Peter Alliss: 'Well, that says it all, Peter.'

KEEP SWINGING

I hope you have enjoyed my wanderings through the world of golf, whether you are good at the game or whether you are amongst the 80 per cent of players who will never achieve a handicap of less than 18; whether you are looking forward to a lifetime of golf or whether much of what I have written in this book has been a trip down Nostalgia Lane.

Golf is currently experiencing a level of growth in many locations worldwide, similar to those which happened in Scotland in the eighteenth century and America in the twentieth. Japan's passion for golf is well known and is now spreading into China, South Korea and even less expected Asian locations like Vietnam. Previously lukewarm golfing countries in Western Europe, like France and Germany, are experiencing a golf boom, which is beginning to extend to eastern European countries like Croatia and Russia. Turkey and Morocco have also entered the fray in the hope of attracting more golf tourists. And golf remains a favourite activity in developed markets like Britain, America, Canada, Australia and South Africa.

After an absence of 112 years, golf will again become an Olympic sport in 2016, on a purpose-built course at Barra da Tijuca in Rio de Janeiro. This Olympic revival may well cause the game to grow exponentially, as many of the 118 member countries of the International Golf Federation suddenly receive government funding to support grass-roots development. A golf explosion is imminent in many parts of the world, perhaps not least in Brazil.

But wherever you are, I hope you continue to enjoy watching and playing the fascinating game that is golf. It will always be a game of highs and lows, and the most important advice I can leave you with is to try and remember always the indisputable philosophy of the legendary Ben Hogan:

The most important shot in golf is the next one.

If you're interested in finding out more about our books, find us on Facebook at **Summersdale Publishers** and follow us on Twitter at **@Summersdale**.

www.summersdale.com

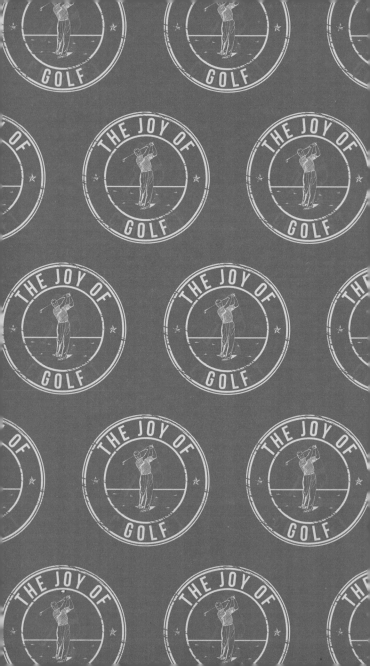